# Dancing
## A Story of Hope for Grieving Hearts

When my significant other Jesse committed suicide two and a half years ago, I was lost and felt I had no other outlets but to dwell in my own guilt. We were together for 16 years. I didn't understand why we had two children. Now they had to go through life fatherless and I was alone so I turned to drinking as a way out and made poor choices. I didn't even recognize myself anymore. I always thought I was a strong individual who took care of my family, but I was so lost. I didn't know what to do. It took me to dark places. Sometimes I thought there was no way out. I believed I had done something really bad to have this happen to me.

I gave my life to the Lord years ago but for some reason I didn't feel God's love. Because I was so numb, I would not open myself up to it. Therefore, I started praying and praying because all I could think about was Jesse's salvation. One early morning in October 2009, the morning star was shining on my house and God gave me peace. At that point I started going back to church praying more and reading my Bible but there was something still missing. I didn't know what it was.

On Mother's Day 2010, my son gave me a book called, _Dancing in the Sky_. I read it and was amazed how inspiring this book was to me. It has helped me in ways I didn't know were possible. My grieving was hindering my relationship with God which was what I was missing. I needed to give Him all my attention and not to my ipod listening to sad songs reminiscing on the past.

When I first lost Jesse my sister used to give me advice. I was so mean to her and would tell her, "You don't know what I am going through unless you have experienced it. If you know someone who has gone through it and come out of it in one piece, and they have the joy and peace in their life that is the person I want to talk to." To be honest I never thought there was a person in this world like that until God brought Yong Hui McDonald in my path. She is an amazing woman and an inspiration to all.

I am so grateful for the book _Dancing in the Sky_. I no longer have that pain in my heart. I am able to talk and share things about Jesse that I was never able to do before without breaking down because I had a big hole in my heart. There is joy now that I never thought I would get. I have been sharing this book with family and friends and anyone who crosses paths with me. God Is amazing and He can heal your broken heart. You gotta give it all to Him. Thank you and God bless!  — Laura Padilla

# ABOUT THE AUTHOR

Yong Hui V. McDonald, also known as Vescinda McDonald, a United Methodist minister, has received her Master of Divinity from The Iliff School of Theology, has been working as a chaplain at Adams County Detention Facility (ACDF) in Brighton, Colorado, since 2003. She is a certified American Correctional Chaplain, spiritual director, author, on-call hospital chaplain, and founder of the Transformation Project Prison Ministry (TPPM) in 2005. TPPM is a 501 (c) (3) non-profit Corporation and produces *Maximum Saints* books and DVDs containing transformation stories of inmates at ACDF. TPPM produced books and DVDs are distributed free of charge in jails, prisons and homeless shelters nationwide. She founded GriefPathway Ventures LLC in 2010 to help others learn how to process grief and healing.

Books Written by Chaplain McDonald:
- *Moment by Moment, I Choose to Love You*
- *Journey With Jesus, Visions, Dreams, Meditations & Reflections*
- *Journey of Mystical Spiritual Experiences*
- *Dancing in the Sky, A Story of Hope for Grieving Hearts*
- *Twisted Logic, The Shadow of Suicide, A Story of Hope for Those Haunted by Suicide or Suicidal Thoughts*
- *Dreams & Interpretations, Healing from Nightmares*
- Compiled and published four *Maximum Saints* books under TPPM and is working on the fifth book called, *Maximum Saints Forgive*.

Devotional books:
- *Reflections* (one week's contribution in 2010), the Upper Room publication,
- An article, "My Cup Overflows" was published in the Korean Christian magazine, "Shinangge" in April, 2006

Producer: Produced the following DVDs:
- Two *Maximum Saints* DVDs
- *Dancing in the Sky, Mismatched Shoes*

# CONTENTS

DEDICATION
ACKNOWLEDGMENTS
INTRODUCTION

## DEDICATION

*I dedicate this book to our Heavenly Father,
my Lord and Savior, Jesus Christ,
the Holy Spirit,
and to my husband
and friend, Keith, with affection and love.*

## "Sense of Beauty"

"Something happened during this grieving process. My sense of beauty has deepened. I see beauty in people, things, and nature more than ever. God has helped me to experience the beauty of people through their good hearts and compassion, which they showed me after I lost my husband. God also has helped me to see beauty in things in which I did not pay much attention before, like nature, furniture, and even color and shape of pillows. Beauty brings healing to me. God created human beings who could feel pain, but also feel beauty to experience healing. Experiencing God's beauty through nature, His unconditional love, and kind people continue to bring healing to my grieving heart."

— Yong Hui V. McDonald

# ACKNOWLEDGMENTS

I thank God for my wonderful mother, for her love and prayers for me. She prays for me and my ministry day and night. I believe because of her prayers God has blessed me and my ministry beyond my imagination. She has been my cheerleader, and I thank God for a wonderful mother who has such love for all her children. She planted the seeds of faith and strength in my heart from my early childhood.

I am also deeply indebted to my wonderful husband, Keith, who passed away in a car accident in 2008, and is with the Lord. He brought healing in my heart and helped my ministry preparation more than anyone I've ever met. I thank God for giving me such a wonderful friend and husband.

I thank the following saints from Adams County Detention Facility (ACDF) for editing this book: Ana Martinez, Crystal Gillespie, Rosalind Cooper, Quiana Hydleburg, Rick Pacheco, Rosa Mendez, Cecilia Medina, Latasha Walker, Alayna Garcia, Nicole Serrat, Jennifer Tilton, Siedah Love, Kara Lounsbury, Cheryl Banks, Doreen Gurule, Elisha Ostmeyer, Wendy Kitchens, Pauline Sanchez, Sharon Gallegos and many more whose names are not in this book. I especially thank Joanne Nobles, a trustee, for helping me with the final editing of this book. In addition, I thank Laura Nokes Lang, Helen Sirios, Jody Nighswonger, Michael Goins, Abigail McKinney, Kitty Lou Rusher, Maxine Morarie, Cassie O'Connor, Sister Maureen Kehoe, Angela Clark and Deann L. Anderson for editing. I thank Sally Shuler for the cover picture.

I appreciate Sara Gallegos for giving me the permission to add her story about Keith in this book.

My sincere thanks also goes out to all of the staff at the ACDF, for their support as well: Sheriff Douglas N. Darr, Lieutenant, Melanie Gregory, Program Coordinator Mr. Sterritt Fuller, and all of the Program Department staff.

Finally, I give glory and thanks to Jesus for giving me the opportunity to share my story of grief and healing. Without Jesus, this book would not have been written.

# INTRODUCTION

## Wonders Beyond Imagination

Keith was the pastor of two churches: Community United Methodist Church in Keenesburg and James Memorial United Methodist Church in Hudson, Colorado. He had been a pastor since 1987 and served eight different churches, and was my husband for nearly 30 years. He died in an automobile accident on July 9, 2008. This book is a journal of the loss, the grief, and God's miraculous healing that made it possible for me to continue His work in prison ministry after Keith's death.

Just before his death, Keith and I had been planning a trip to Montana for the McDonald family reunion, which was to be held on July 17, 2008. Keith was very excited that I would be going with him this year – I had missed the reunion the year before to visit my mother in Los Angeles. This year we planned to visit our daughter, Nicole, in Buffalo, Wyoming, on the way to the reunion. From Montana I would fly to Los Angeles to visit my mom, and Keith would spend one more week vacationing by himself. Five days before we were to leave for Buffalo, he died.

Keith's death was totally unexpected. However, God had asked me to listen to Him in silence for a couple of months before the accident. When I try to listen to God, my heart is attentive to the people around me. That was what happened with Keith - I was able to listen and enjoy being with him more just before he died.

I had experienced the grief that accompanies the loss of someone close to me twice before: my father's suicide and my younger sister's death at the age of 18 in a car accident. I expected that losing a spouse would be different somehow, but I had no idea how I would react or how long it would take to recover. Part of my training as a minister is helping people grieve the loss of their loved ones. I thought I knew what I had to do to help myself, but I learned something new in my grieving for Keith – that God can, and does, lead us step-by-step to a healed heart.

I have been journaling for many years, but after Keith died I tried to focus on three areas: (1) general journaling of my reflections, dreams, visions, and my walk with God; (2) documenting what makes me cry and break down with grief and loss; (3) what brings healing to my heart.

It has been six months since Keith died. I could not be writing this if God had not healed my broken heart, which is now filled with joy and peace. The Holy Spirit guided this book project and directed me to add a Prayer Project to help people who are grieving and are in need of healing.

My prayer is that by sharing my path of pain, grief, and healing, you will also experience healing in your own life, and know the love and power of God in your deepest trouble.

*Dancing in the Sky*

# Part One: A Story of Hope for Grieving Hearts

## Chapter One: Crossing the River of Tears

### 1. Unexpected Death (7-9-2008)

July 9, 2008, was my day off. I was doing house chores, and Keith was working on the computer, preparing his e-mail devotion for his congregations. Around noon, Keith asked me if I could take pictures of him riding a recently-purchased recumbent bike. He was going to include the picture in his e-mail devotion.

I took many pictures of him riding the bike in front of our home. Keith's excitement about his new bike made me happy. Every time Keith had a new hobby he was always excited. This excitement and joyful heart rubbed off on everyone around him. This was certainly one of those times.

That evening, Keith and I were planning to attend a Special Olympics fundraising dinner at the Adams County Fairgrounds at 6:30. Keith would teach a Tae Kwon Do class and finish by 5:30 p.m. I had been asked to pray before the meal. I had an uneasy feeling that if we went together I might be late, so we decided to drive separately. I left home early and went to the Adams County Fairgrounds.

Keith still wasn't there after the dinner started. He did not answer his cell phone. I looked at the door many times, but he never showed up. I had an empty feeling, and I was missing him the whole time. I couldn't understand why he wasn't there. If he said he would be there, he always showed up. I thought that perhaps he may have finished Tae Kwon Do so late and had decided not to come.

Around 8:30 p.m. while I was driving home, I saw two police cars with their lights on at Hwy 85 and 144th Ave., in Brighton, which wasn't far from the fairgrounds. I realized there had been a car accident.

When I got home, I saw a police car parked in front of our home and two police officers standing outside. I rolled down the window and asked if there was anything wrong. After I got out of the car, they asked me if Keith was my husband. I said, "Yes." They told me that Keith had been in a car accident in Brighton that morning, and was sent to Denver Health. I told them that they had the wrong person since my husband was at home until late that afternoon. They checked his name and told me that indeed it was my husband.

First, I thought Keith had gotten into a minor accident. He had never had an accident in our 30 years of our marriage. While we were talking, the police officer got a call, and then he told me Keith had passed away. I was in shock. All I could say was, "I cannot believe it, I cannot believe it." I immediately called Keith's parents in Missoula, Montana, and told them the news. The officers asked me if there was anyone who could drive me to Denver Health. My friend Helen and her son drove me to the hospital. I called my daughter, Nicole, and told her the news, then called my son, Fletcher, but he did not answer.

I phoned Rev. Loren Boyce, the associate director of Mission and Ministry of the Rocky Mountain Conference of the United Methodist Church, and told him Keith had died, so we would have to cancel the DVD project we were planning. The next morning he was scheduled to come to Adams County Detention Facility (ACDF) to video tape the testimony of inmates to help the youth. Loren called Bishop Warner Brown and Rev. Youngsook Kang, my district superintendent. They both immediately called me to offer support. When Rev. Kang asked if she could come to the hospital for support, I told her that my family would handle the situation.

When we arrived at Denver Health, my friends Jody and David were there, looking dazed. We were all in shock. A social worker told me what happened to Keith. He was turning left across 144th Ave. and Hwy 85 in Brighton, was hit by an oncoming car with such force that his truck rolled, and was thrown out of the vehicle. He always wore his seat belt, but this did not help him. The vehicle landed on him, and had to be moved. There was no sign of life, but they did CPR and got Keith's pulse back. After that, they flew him to Denver Health. In the Emergency Room, despite the effort of the medical team, Keith showed no signs of life. They stopped trying to revive him, and was pronounced dead at 7:58 p.m. The hospital told me he died from internal bleeding.

I told the social worker I wanted to see Keith's body. She told me his body had already been sent to the Adams County Coroner. When I called the coroner's office, they told me they had not received Keith's body yet, so I asked the social worker where his body was. After she spoke with the supervisors, she told me that Keith was in the morgue. I told them I would like to see him. The hospital nurse told me that they would not let anyone go to the morgue. I said I would like to see him in a viewing room, but they told me they did not have one. They handed me Keith's cross and a few things that he had carried. His wallet and cell phone were missing.

The hospital where I work has a viewing room. The first thing a hospital should do is let the family see the deceased, no matter what the condition. I wanted to see his body before he went to the coroner for an

*Dancing in the Sky*

autopsy. I was very frustrated. I asked the social worker to find out if there was any way I could see my husband's body. The hospital told me that the coroner was on the way to pick him up, and I could see the body in a warehouse within 30 minutes. They would let me know where that would be.

I called Fletcher again, but he did not answer. My friends took me to his apartment which was not far from the hospital. Fletcher was in shock when he heard the news, and came to the hospital with me.

While we were waiting at the hospital, a nurse warned me that Keith was plugged with a tube and we needed to be prepared. I remembered how awful people look with a tube in their throat and needles stuck in their body. Many times families of the deceased have asked me to remove the tubes because it looks horrible, but I have to tell them that until the coroner releases the body the hospital can't remove them. The hospital needs to show that they did everything they could to revive the person. Because my husband died in an accident, I knew that the coroner would be involved and would do an autopsy to find out the cause of death.

In the end, I told the nurse I did not want to see Keith's body with a tube in his throat. I did not want to remember him in that condition. Fletcher also declined to see Keith's body after I explained to him how horrible he might look.

After taking Fletcher to his apartment, Jody and David took me home around 1:30 a.m. They asked me if I would be all right alone. I told them I would be. I walked into the house empty-hearted, shocked, and in tears. It was hard to accept the fact that Keith would never be with me in that house again. I was pretty shaken, not knowing how rough my journey would be. There was no guessing how life would be without Keith, since he had been a part of my life for so long. I knew many more tears would follow as I entered the doorway to grief and sorrow. There was no way to escape this path. I had to walk through it alone, but did not know how long I had to walk it or how long I would have to shed my tears.

In the midst of turmoil and feeling lost, God started healing my heart by giving me the understanding that Keith had lived a full life. Life is fragile. If it wasn't Keith's time, he would have survived. This understanding was difficult to handle, especially the first day after Keith died. But I was familiar with God's voice, so I accepted the fact that even though Keith was only 50 years old, he had lived life to the fullest. Accepting Keith's death from the beginning of this grieving process helped me tremendously. It was a terrible loss for me, our family, and the many people who loved him. Yet, God did not allow me to doubt His grace in this tragedy.

## 2. God's Grace  (7-10-2008)

Early in the morning, I canceled my husband's cell phone since I did not know where it was. I went to the Brighton Police Station to talk to the police officer who attended Keith's accident so I could hear more about what happened, but he wasn't on duty. The police station did not know what happened to Keith's wallet and his cell phone. I told them that I would like to go to the towing company to see his truck and pick up his belongings.

I went to the insurance company to notify them of the accident and called the towing company. They told me I needed an accident report, the title for the truck, and the towing fee before they would release anything. When I saw the truck I couldn't believe my eyes. It was crushed on the right side and almost unrecognizable.

I took many pictures of the truck and started gathering Keith's stuff, which was scattered all over. I couldn't believe that Keith was dead. I just couldn't stop my tears. After that, I went to the accident scene and picked up some of the church papers that were on the ground. I looked everywhere, but couldn't find his wallet and cell phone. That afternoon, the coroner's office called saying that they had Keith's wallet, cell phone, and wedding ring.

I met Fletcher for lunch at a restaurant, but we were in such shock that we did not have much to say. I said, "I feel bad that I wasn't with him to help him. Maybe I could have helped him prevent the accident if I had been with him." Fletcher replied, "No, Mom, don't say that. You could have also died if you were with him." Fletcher could be right since I usually did not pay attention to Keith's driving, because I trusted his driving.

After Fletcher went back to his apartment, I went home and spoke with my mother-in-law and father-in-law on the phone. We decided to have the funeral on July 17. All of our family would be coming for the funeral, and I knew I had to clean the house. Keith and I were messy all the time, so we did not complain to each other, but now I had no choice but to clean.

As I started to clean, I was not in a good mood because cleaning is not one of my gifts. I had to pick up loads of Keith's clothes from the floor to do the laundry. I said, "Why didn't he pick up his clothes?" God said, "It's God's grace that you are doing Keith's laundry for the last time. He would have done the same for you.

Someone else will have to clean your stuff someday. If both of you could not help, your children would be cleaning up all the stuff. It's God's grace that you can help others and your husband."

With that, I started thanking God every time I picked up Keith's clothes and other belongings and said, "Thank you, God. Thank you for your grace. Thank you for helping me clean Keith's stuff." I no longer had a grumbling spirit. Keith was independent and did all of his own laundry and cooked for himself and for the family. In fact, he purchased most of our dishes and silverware, and each time I saw them it reminded me of Keith and made me sad. God reminded me that it was a privilege to be married to Keith. He was a good husband. I remembered one day when I was upset with Keith, God asked me if I had seen a husband who was better than my husband. My answer was no. Keith was an amazing person, though we had many challenges.

In 1978, God told me to ask Pastor Kim to find a man for me to marry. I went and talked to him. On January 5, 1978, he introduced me to Keith who was in the Air Force, stationed at Osan Air Base in Songtan, Korea, where I lived. Keith was attending Pastor Kim's church and I was attending Suwon Bible College at the time. Keith and I decided to get married the first day we met. We both believed that God led us to meet. I had asked God to help me find a husband who loved God. Keith loved God, and I was amazed by his interest in studying the Bible. I had never met anyone like him. I felt like he was my husband even before we were married. I've never felt like that with anyone else. It was as if I already knew him. That was a confirmation from the Lord that he indeed was the answer to my prayer. Our love was not at first sight. Our love grew as we spent time together. We both loved to study the Bible and that's the reason we attended Multnomah Bible College together. I felt privileged to have someone who could carry on a theological conversation with me. He had high moral standards, and I never doubted his faithfulness. However, we faced challenges when I decided to go into the ministry because he wanted my support as a pastor's wife.

As I look back, God was preparing my heart all along. He prepared me to be independent by calling me to ministry. Keith prepared me to do the same by not allowing me to rely on him. At times, I was resentful when Keith would not help me. When I asked his opinion about different matters he wouldn't tell me what he thought, but told me to make the decision by myself. It got to the point that I went out and bought a car, in my name, without asking his opinion. He was okay with that! Keith liked my independent spirit and even pushed me to do the tax preparation. Now, I'm thankful for that, because I see how it helps me. After Keith died, my immediate concern was to find a new house because we lived in a parsonage. That was extremely difficult for me, since the home Keith and I lived in the last six years had suddenly become a temporary rental home. I felt pressure to find a place and there was little time to prepare for the change.

A month before Keith's accident I had had a dream that I was alone and had to move because there was a new owner of the house in which I was living. I had made some changes, and the new owner was nice about it. I did not realize how prophetic the dream was, until now. I started reading Proverbs and God's Word ministered to me. It says, *"Trust in the Lord with all your heart and lean not on your own understanding; in all your ways acknowledge him, and he will make your paths straight." (Proverbs 3:5-6)* I asked God to bring healing to my grieving heart.

### 3. Reflection (7-11-2008)

Keith wanted to be cremated, but I did not have the heart to call funeral homes to find a reasonable one. I called Helen and she offered to call for me. When Helen called back, she told me that Stoddard Funeral Home in Greeley was willing to do the service free of charge. That was great news since I struggled to come up with money for funeral expenses.

It was a long day at the funeral home, but I was comforted by John Rutledge, the funeral director, who was so caring and compassionate. When I thanked him for doing Keith's funeral for free, he said, "We loved Keith, and he contributed so much to the community. It's time that we take care of him." I thanked God for their generosity.

Rev. Eric Smith, Keith's district superintendent, came. He would conduct the funeral service. He was very supportive of me and my family. The funeral home would take care of the funeral bulletin and the obituaries. The obituaries will be sent to five newspapers in different states where Keith had served as pastor. Since Keith wanted cremation, the funeral home would provide the large urn free of charge. I purchased four small urns: one for Keith's parents, one each for Nicole and Fletcher, and one for me.

Before he passed away, Keith had been organizing a food pantry called "Loaves and Fishes" with Father Frank Garcia from Holy Family Catholic Church. I decided that the memorial funds should go to the food pantry.

Since Keith had written his funeral service, Eric asked me to find it so he could make the service arrangements. That night I checked all of Keith's computer files in his study, but I couldn't find his funeral service folder. I almost gave up. Finally, I asked God to help me find it. Soon afterwards, I found it in our bedroom. I couldn't find the original computer disk, so I had to type the whole thing. Keith had a long sermon about a jumping mouse. That was one of his favorite stories. He told me it described a Christian's spiritual journey of transformation. It was about 5:00 a.m. when I finished typing.

I asked, "Would I marry Keith again?" My answer was yes. I loved him, and I still love him. I loved him more than any other human being. I felt so lucky to marry someone that I loved so much. I have no doubt that Keith is with God where there is no pain, no tears, no suffering, but filled with peace and joy. I prayed, "Thank you, Lord. Keith was a good husband and I was thankful to meet him. I would marry him again if I were to live again."

## 4. A Dream (7-12-2008)

I asked God to show me if He was taking care of Keith. God answered my prayers. I had a dream that night and saw Keith standing in front of me, bowing to me, and then he said, "Thank you." I heard his voice as if I were hearing it when I was awake. Then, he disappeared. I thanked God for Keith's visit for He had shown me that Keith was doing fine.

One of my favorite Bible verses comes from the book of John. Jesus said, *"Do not let your hearts be troubled. Trust in God; trust also in me. In my Father's house are many rooms; if it were not so, I would have told you. I am going there to prepare a place for you. And if I go and prepare a place for you, I will come back and take you to be with me that you also may be where I am. You know the way to the place where I am going.' Thomas said to him, 'Lord, we don't know where you are going, so how can we know the way?' Jesus answered, 'I am the way and the truth and the life. No one comes to the Father except through me.'"* (John 14:1-6) What more can I ask from God? Jesus prepared a room for Keith, and he is already in a heavenly home with Jesus. I am thankful that God has plans for those who believe. I will be able to see Keith some day when I arrive in heaven. That gives me hope. I wrote a letter to Keith after I woke up from this dream at 5:24 a.m.

Dearest Keith,

I love you. I will always love you. Thank you for all the joy you brought in my life for the last 30 years. You were a wonderful husband, father, grandfather and a friend to many others who knew you. Even after you died, because of you, I'm being taken care of by many. Your visit in my dream has helped me immensely and gave me comfort and peace. I thank you for your understanding and your love. I thank God whenever I think about you because He is taking care of you. I have no doubt that you will wait for me and pray for me because life here is more challenging than yours. I can see your smile. You may be dancing with Jesus - even though you did not like dancing when you were on earth. You may be saying, "Why did I exercise so much? Heaven is too good." Well, I miss you, but I know you are in a good place with God. I told you this before, but I will say it again. If I were to live again, I would marry you again. Thank you for your love. I'll always have you in my heart. The thing I miss the most is your enthusiasm and sense of humor. I remember you ordered brown contact lenses and told me that I had brown eyes and our children had brown eyes, and you wanted to look like us. You even sang "Beautiful Brown Eyes" and that made me feel special. I believe others in heaven will be enjoying your presence and your sense of humor. I am thankful that I was married to you, and I thank you for putting up with me.

Your wife forever,

Yong Hui

## 5. Idolizing  (7-13-2008)

When I went to pick up Keith's stuff, I picked up the shirt and tie that he was wearing the night of the accident. The shirt had blood spots on it. I was going to keep it to show to my family so they could have closure. I left it on Keith's bathroom counter, and just before I went to sleep the Holy Spirit spoke to me that I should let go of the past, especially painful memories of my husband's accident and death.

Somehow I felt I should not grieve. Why? If I saw everything in God's eyes I should not grieve over the loss of Keith. If I truly believe that Keith is in heaven with God and he is happy, there is no reason to grieve. But, I focused on what I did not have and was clinging to what I was missing. God helped me to realize that I cannot idolize the belongings of people. In this case, it was the last thing Keith wore. I felt God was telling me to let go. I threw them into the garbage can. I prayed, "Thank you God for helping me to realize that my focus cannot be on idolizing what Keith had, but my focus should be on you."

The lesson of letting go of Keith's belongings took a long time. When I was trying to decide which clothes I should give to the funeral home for Keith's cremation, I couldn't let go of Keith's favorite western suit and shirt. He wore it on many special occasions. I wasn't going to give it to anyone. I could not bear the thought of not being able to see them, so I kept them. I gave them Keith's clerical robe and a western shirt for his final clothes. Within three months, I ended up giving away all of his clothes. I went through a period when I was holding on to everything and anything that Keith had worked on. Eventually, God helped me to let go of a lot of the belongings and attachments I had to them. It was the only way that I could move on and not hold on to the past and be frozen with grief and pain.

## 6. Resurrection (7-14-2008)

When God has lessons for me, He sometimes speaks to me through Scripture as soon as I wake up, and that's what He did this particular morning. The lessons were about resurrection. *"He is not here; he has risen, just as he said. Come and see the place where he lay." (Matthew 28:6) "Jesus said to her, 'I am the resurrection and the life. He who believes in me will live, even though he dies; and whoever lives and believes in me will never die. Do you believe this?'" (John 11:25-26)* I was greatly encouraged. God was reminding me that Keith is not dead, but his spirit is alive. The Christian message of hope and resurrection is so real. Keith is not here. He has risen. I believe when a person dies he or she is with the Lord if he or she is a Christian.

My daughter arrived with her three daughters, and I enjoyed spending time with them. I asked Nicole to help me select Keith's pictures for the funeral home so they could prepare a slide presentation for the funeral service. She also helped me pack and clean the house. She was so organized. I was so thankful that she came to help me. Her husband, John, had to work and was planning to come before the funeral.

Nicole said she wanted to see Keith's body. I told her I wasn't sure what Keith would look like after the accident and autopsy. I felt I would have to be mindful of my children's grieving process. Maybe

Nicole would want to see Keith's shirt and tie that he wore for the last time. It might help her grieving process. I took them out of the garbage and put them in Keith's bathroom in case my children wanted to look at them. She kept insisting on seeing his body, so I made arrangements. We had to see his body as soon as possible, since they were going to send him to the crematory the next day.

I went to the funeral home to view Keith's body that afternoon with Nicole. The funeral home was very nice about the last-minute notice. They did not charge anything for the viewing. Keith had a bruise on the left side of his head and his skin was pale. Other than that, since he was wearing robes and a red stole, he did not look bad. I couldn't help but cry, "I'm so sorry, Keith. Thank you, God, for taking care of Keith." That's all I could say. I touched his hands and face for the last time. He was cold. God reminded me of the Scripture, *"He has risen. He is not here."* ( *Mark 16:6)* How appropriate that Scripture was. God had prepared me for this moment. Fletcher arrived to see Keith's body. He was crying when he came into the room where Keith was. I spent more time with Keith, alone, and cried some more, and then we left. I was glad that Nicole insisted that we see him.

That evening the Holy Family Catholic Church priest, Father Frank Garcia, who was kind and compassionate, organized a prayer vigil at the fairgrounds in Keenesburg to remember Keith. It was like a memorial service. Different people shared their memories of Keith. It was comforting and encouraging for me to see many of my good friends. I was touched by the service. It made me cry. After the service, many people came and showed their concern and their care. Holy Family Church provided the food.

Holy Family, Community UMC, and James Memorial UMC brought food and encouraged me. The Spiritual Care department from my hospital sent a fruit basket. My friends asked me how they could help. I told them they could help me clean my house and get ready for the funeral. Karla and Jody helped clean, delivered furniture to a thrift shop, and took out the garbage.

Paul said, *"Carry each other's burdens, and in this way you will fulfill the law of Christ." (Galatians 6:2)* Many carried my burdens during my grieving process, and they brought so much healing to my heart. I cannot express my gratitude to all who showed their love and concern. Their prayers carried me through my days of pain and suffering.

## 7. Concerns  (7-15-2008)

When Keith passed away, the immediate concern for me was to find a place to live. I understood that when a pastor dies, according to the United Methodist Discipline, the spouse has a month to move out of the parsonage. I thought it would be impossible for me, since I did not have a place to go. I had to sort and discard a lot of stuff that we had accumulated over the last 30 years. I told the church that it would be three months before I could move. I started asking friends if they knew of someone's home I could rent.

I began worrying about all of the new expenses. It was nice that the church told me that they would not charge me for July, but starting in August, I needed to start paying $1,050 for rent and utilities. The church owed Keith more than $2,000 for professional expenses and told me I probably wouldn't owe them anything. They were right. After I moved, I received a check for the remaining balance of Keith's professional expenses. Up until Keith's death, the church also paid for our family's health insurance. They told me that starting in August I would have to pay for my family's health insurance.

The Lord knew my concerns. This morning, I opened the Bible, to Hebrews 13:5-6: *"Keep your lives free from the love of money and be content with what you have, because God has said, 'Never will I leave you; never will I forsake you.' So we say with confidence, 'The Lord is my helper; I will not be afraid. What can man do to me?'"* I was thankful that God would take care of me.

## 8. Comfort  (7-16-2008)

Tomorrow is the funeral and the Adams County Sheriff's Department brought a lot of food: meat, bread, mayonnaise, fruit trays, crackers, cheese, and drinks. Candi, the library assistant, brought it in a big cooler. The food was for my family who would be coming from different states to attend the funeral. That made me happy. They truly showed that they care. Sheriff Douglas Darr called me and asked how I was doing and told me he would be coming to the funeral. I was touched by his kind, encouraging words.

Pastor Yolanda Garcia, from All Access Church, came and helped me clean the living room, kitchen, and refrigerator. I was so thankful for her kindness.

I went to visit a possible rental. A woman owned the home and charged $700 a month for the basement, which included utilities. I knew I could not live with someone when I visited her. I needed more privacy, so decided to look into buying a home.

I went shopping with Nicole and my granddaughters to buy clothes for the funeral. I did not have time to pick up my sister, Son Hui, from the airport. Jody had volunteered to pick her up if I got too busy. I called Jody and she picked her up for me. I called Karla to let her know that my house wasn't ready and it needed cleaning. When I arrived home, Karla and others came and cleaned my house and set the table. It was so clean. I was so thankful for my friends.

My mother-in-law, Bernice, father-in-law, Desmond, sister-in-law, Jeaneane, and her husband, Mark, their daughter, Mariah, my brother-in-law, Kevin, and his wife, Sara, came to my home. Jeaneane told me that she wanted to see Keith's body. I told her that I had decided not to have Keith's body at the funeral service since Keith did not seem to like viewing the dead bodies. I told her it was too late because Keith was already cremated, but will have his ashes at the funeral the next morning.

It was good that Nicole took Keith's last pictures at the funeral home. We all sat and watched Keith's final pictures and reminisced about his life. Even though it was a sad occasion, there was plenty of laughter as we remembered the good times with him. It was so comforting to have all of my family there. I told them that I kept Keith's last shirt and tie from the accident, and they were on his bathroom counter. I told them that the shirt had some blood spots on it, but if anyone wanted to see them they could. Nicole said she already saw them. I asked Jeaneane and Kevin if they wanted to see them. They said no.

That evening, I had a dream about Keith. He was making a funny face to make me laugh. I started laughing, then woke up and said, "Thank you, God, for Keith's humor!"

## 9. A Funeral (7-17-2008)

Dr. Dennis and Laurie Yutani came from Wyoming to attend the funeral. They were our close friends, and I was glad that they were able to come. Dennis and Keith did Tae Kwon Do together whenever Keith could stop by Dennis' home. Our family and Dennis' family did Tae Kwon Do together in Glasgow, Montana. My son-in-law, John, came with his parents. Nicole, John, his parents, and Fletcher helped me clean the garage. They were such a big help.

The church people thought that there would not be enough room in the church for all the guests and decided to have the service at Weld Central High School in Keenesburg. They were expecting about 300 people, but about 500 people attended the funeral service. There were more than 30 pastors from the Rocky Mountain and Yellowstone Conferences of the United Methodist Church. Many deputies, program staff and volunteers from ACDF, as well as hospital chaplains came.

The slideshow presentation of Keith's life was beautifully done and was touching. I couldn't stop my tears, remembering all the good times our family had, especially with our kids. It was a beautiful way of celebrating Keith's life. Sara, a youth representative from Community UMC, Matthew from First UMC of Buffalo, Wyoming, and other pastors participated in the service of the Jumping Mouse story. People laughed as they remembered Keith's humor. At the end of the service, my granddaughters, Teila and Jamie, and my niece, Mariah, released my husband's pigeons.

The McDonald family was going to have a family reunion on July 17 at Swan Lake in Montana, but it turned out be Keith's funeral instead. It was a sad day, yet I was glad that all of his family was able to come. Keith would have been pleased to see how many people missed and loved him.

The churches provided a luncheon at the fairgrounds. Bill Dale, who was Keith's pharmacist, told me about a dream he had had. In his dream, people gathered for Keith's funeral service. Suddenly, Keith burst through the back door and said, "It was just a joke. I just wanted to see how many would show up for my funeral." Then, people gathered around him and there were laughter and tears, and they hugged him. Somehow, no one was upset with him about his joke. It was a joyful occasion. When Bill shared this dream, everyone laughed, including my mother-in-law and father-in-law. We all agreed that Keith was one who could joke like that.

That night my sister, Son Hui, cooked dinner at home. Everyone loved the Korean food, and there was a lot of laughter even though we were all still in shock. Fletcher brought the accident report. I was thankful that he picked it up when I did not ask him to do so. After that, we all drove to see Keith's truck, took more pictures, and went to the place where the accident had been.

Jeaneane gave me a book, _Healing a Spouse's Grieving Heart_, a photo album of Keith and his family from the previous year's family reunion. She has always been so thoughtful. I was grateful for her thoughtfulness. Nicole and John left with their kids that evening. The McDonald family planned to stay one more day.

10. My Father-In-Law (7-18-2008)

I asked my father-in-law and mother-in-law to take Keith's

ashes to Montana. When the McDonald family gets together in 2009, we can bury his ashes next to his brother Marvin, who died in a climbing accident in the Grand Tetons. Before my father-in-law left, he told me to call him if I needed anything. He said it twice, and I knew he meant it. After my father-in-law left, Son Hui mentioned how much he cared about me to say that twice. It made me choke up with tears. I knew I was loved and being taken care of by many people.

That night, I saw a full moon. Keith and I used to debate about full moons. He did not like them because he felt a full moon caused a lot of trouble for people. I said full moons were beautiful because God created them and they give more light. Keith would learn to enjoy all the creations in heaven, including full moons. God spoke to me, "My daughter, I will be taking care of you, so don't worry. I am taking care of your husband as well. You shouldn't worry about him."

All the flowers donated to Keith's funeral were in my home. They were beautiful and I especially liked what Hyon Bohnenkamp made. She has a floral shop and I am always amazed by her gifts. Her flowers reminded me of what happened while I was leading a Prayer and Meditation at Samaritan House, a homeless shelter in Denver. I was playing music for meditation. I asked the people around the table to picture that they were walking on a path somewhere with Jesus and have a conversation with him. That day God gave me a vision I will never forget. I was walking with Jesus in a field of flowers. Jesus told me he would give me all the flowers and I asked, "Really?" He replied, "Of course. I even gave you my life, didn't I?" A couple days after I had this vision, Hyon made a beautiful flower arrangement for me. I knew where it was coming from. Jesus was giving me flowers through Hyon. After this experience, when people give me something to make me happy, I know who is behind it. Also, when I give something to others, many times it is not initiated by me, but it is the Lord telling me to give.

The flowers Hyon gave me were very beautiful, and I wanted to share them with others, so I started taking them to ACDF chaplain's worship services, and many inmates appreciated them. For many years, Hyon has donated flowers and plants for chaplain's worship services. She is one of the most giving and generous people that I know.

## 11. Hobbies and Interests  (7-19-2008)

Everyone left except Son Hui. I was reminiscing with her about Keith's life. I told her that I was glad that Keith did what he wanted to do. He was creative and had many hobbies, pets, and interests.

For the last 12 years, he raised homing pigeons in a loft. I took many rides with him, when he trained the birds. He would let them go at weddings and funerals, the birds would come back home. No other pastor had done that, and so many people appreciated it. It was great to see the birds flying in the sky from our backyard.

Keith bought a one-person kayak. He loved it so much that he bought a two-person kayak for our wedding anniversary. I loved kayaking with him.

After we moved to Keenesburg, he bought a malamute, Bradley, and trained her to pull a dog cart. I went on many rides with Keith. Wherever we went, people looked at us because a dog cart is not something you usually see in a park. He decided to get another malamute, Jaffa, so he could pull with Bradley, but Keith died before Jaffa was old enough to pull.

Keith was fascinated by koi fish, so he built a koi pond. He was very proud of it. Many times Keith asked me to feed the fish with him. It was fun to watch them. Unfortunately, all the fish died last winter when the pump broke. There was no circulation in the water, so the fish froze to death. Keith was so depressed, it took a long time for him to clean the pond. He was going to fix the pump, but he never got to it.

His hobbies kept increasing, and his most recent hobby was riding a recumbent bike. He offered to let me ride it, but I didn't. He loved Tae Kwon Do and practiced almost every day. He taught Tae Kwon Do when we lived in Buffalo and here in Keenesburg. He bought a lot of equipment so he could teach kids free of charge, and had a fun time demonstrating it to me.

In recent years, he got into swordsmanship and he tried to teach me, but I did not get into it. Also, he liked throwing darts and he offered to let me try. I wasn't interested, so I would just sit and watch him.

Keith was brilliant with language studies. He had studied German in high school and wanted to go to Germany to use his skills. He learned Korean in the military. They sent him to Korea. Keith majored in Greek and Hebrew when he attended Multnomah Bible College. He translated the Gospel of Mark from Greek to English, and he was so proud of it. He continuously studied Korean, Chinese, and Spanish. One day Keith gave me a wall hanging on which he wrote, "I love you forever" in Korean, Chinese and English. That meant a lot to me.

Our children loved Keith's creativity. They had so much fun with him when they were little. Whenever he was on a trip, Keith always bought interesting gifts for our kids, which made them happy.

One day, I wanted to see how our children felt about their parents. We had no intention of divorcing, but I asked Fletcher and Nicole which parent they wanted to be with if we were to divorce. They said they wanted to live with Keith because he was fun.

I am glad that I did not complain about Keith's growing hobbies. Instead, I enjoyed life with him. As I realize now, life is short and it's good to have fun. I was focused on ministry. Still, I appreciated Keith's different hobbies, because I could spend time with him and enjoy life. My sister and I agreed that Keith enjoyed life even though his family life and ministry were challenging.

Son Hui and I went to look at some houses. Keith and I had discussed the future home we wanted to buy. Some of the new houses we looked at were beautiful. I couldn't stop thinking of how great it would be if Keith could share the house with me. I couldn't find anything that I liked well enough to buy.

After I took my sister to the airport, I went home and tried to rest, but I couldn't. I was crying and I still couldn't believe Keith had died. I tried to convince myself that Keith was in a better place than I am, so I didn't have to grieve, but that didn't work. I prayed to God to give me strength in this journey of grieving so I could experience healing. I started looking at photo albums, and I couldn't stop my tears. But, I knew God had prepared me for this. I knew somehow He would help me get through it. I just didn't know how long it would take me to heal from this loss. Thank you, God, for preparing me for this. Lord, you are so great!

When I started looking to buy a house, many possibilities went through my mind. Maybe I could buy a home and have homeless Korean women live with me. A Korean-American United Methodist Church woman pastor had started one like that. In fact, I visited their home in St. Louis and was amazed by what they were doing. Seven homeless women lived in the house. The pastor who started it wasn't there at the time, so they put me in her room for the night. I left that place in tears because I was so touched by them. I knew there was no way I could be involved with a homeless ministry. I wouldn't have any time to take care of them because I am too busy with the prison ministry. I knew I needed to pray about it.

Earlier this year, God confronted me and said that I needed to choose one: either love God or love the ministry. I was surprised by that request. The first time He asked me was during worship, and I couldn't make the decision. Then, when he asked me the second time, I finally realized what was happening. I had misunderstood what it meant to

*Dancing in the Sky*

love God. I thought loving the ministry was loving God. I found joy in serving God, and when I was so focused on serving God, I neglected spending time with God in prayer. I was to love God first, and then love the ministry. But, I fell in love with the prison ministry and started thinking that spending time in the ministry was spending time with God. God proved to me that I was wrong. God even spoke to me through Scripture.

When a woman anointed Jesus with perfume and tears, others thought she should have sold the perfume and given the money to the poor. Jesus replied, *"You will always have the poor among you, but you will not always have me." (John 12:8)* Jesus spoke to my heart, "You will always have prisoners, but you will not always have me unless you learn to focus your heart to spend time with me."

When I finally told God that I had chosen to love Him and that He would be my first priority, I felt Father God on my left and the Holy Spirit on my right. That was such a glorious experience that I knew I had made the right decision. I thanked God in tears.

Since then, God has told me to spend more time with Jesus in prayer. I know whatever I do, even good things, I have to put aside if they hinder my time with the Lord. I prayed, "Lord, I need your guidance because my ministry cannot be my first priority. Help me so I don't neglect spending time with you. Lord, help me to love you more. I need your wisdom."

As I thought about it more, starting a homeless shelter was out of the question. I am not allowed to work with inmates when they leave the facility. Many homeless people are ex-inmates. I feel my calling is to work inside a jail. I have to let others do the work outside. Again, I felt there would be many ministry opportunities if I could open my house to others, but Jesus had to come first. I need God's wisdom on that because my first focus has to be spending time with God. In addition, I am a private person and I need a lot of time to be alone with God.

I will miss Keith's presence, but I believe he is happier with God because there is no pain in heaven. Jesus can give happiness beyond measure. In this life he suffered from hip pain from the beginning of our marriage. Tae Kwon Do helped him, but he still had to take pain medication. The Scripture from the book of Revelation encouraged me. *"And I heard a loud voice from the throne saying, 'Now the dwelling of God is with men, and he will live with them. They will be his people, and God himself will be with them and be their God. He will wipe every tear from their eyes. There will be no more death or mourning or crying or pain, for the old order of things has passed away.'" (Revelation 21:3-4)*

## 12. Forgiveness (7-20-2008)

It has been 11 days since Keith passed away. I knew I wasn't ready to go back to work, but I went to ACDF to check my e-mail and visit Deputy Sheri Duran, my good friend. She was so supportive of me in many ways, and just talking with her has helped me immensely. I thank God for her. After I arrived home, I started reflecting on my life with Keith. I have many good memories of him. He brought so much healing in my life. In fact, I thanked God for Keith many times. But, there were challenging times because he was against my decision to go into the ministry. Keith supported everything I wanted to do, so it was a surprise that he would try to discourage me. He wanted me to have an independent spirit, but not to the extent that I would pursue ministry. I had to forgive him for that.

I also asked God to help Keith forgive me for all the challenges that I brought to him while he was alive. I was thankful that Keith was more supportive of my ministry in recent years and recognized my gifts. On one occasion, one of his parishioners had a son incarcerated at ACDF. While he was at the jail, he read and was touched by the book, *Maximum Saints Never Hide in the Dark*. It was the first book of ACDF inmate leaders' transformation stories in Christ. He wrote to his mother to get a copy of the book and read it. My husband asked me for a copy of the book and said, "Yong Hui, you did a great job!" I was thankful for that affirmation. I knew God would eventually change his heart, and he did.

I had to forgive Keith and let go of all my resentment about our disputes over how to discipline our children. I told God I forgive Keith. I did it one by one in tears. Keith loved our kids and was good with our kids when they were little, but when they became rebellious teenagers, he couldn't handle them well. He had a short temper and that hurt our kids more than anything. Nicole reconciled with Keith after she met John. I'm so thankful for Nicole's forgiving heart.

Keith and Fletcher were not on good terms for a while. After Fletcher came back from a Korean mission trip, his attitude toward his dad changed. Fletcher made an effort to build a better relationship with his dad by spending time with him. I was thankful for that. Fletcher went back to school and was doing well. Keith and I were proud of our son. I was glad that Keith was able to see the goodness in Fletcher. On 4th of July weekend, Fletcher came home to spend time with him.

*Dancing in the Sky*

Keith even bought a computer for Fletcher and that made me really happy. They had a great time together. Keith died five days later.

## 13. My children (7-21-2008)

Laura Nokes Lang helps me with the fundraising events for the Transformation Project Prison Ministry (TPPM). She told me that I needed to keep talking about my feelings and my grief from losing Keith. She told me to find someone who would listen to my feelings. If they got tired of listening, then find someone else. It sounded humorous to me at the time and I laughed. She understood that healing from grief takes time. It is important to find people who will understand my need to talk about hurts and pains. She gave me good advice because she too had lost her husband. She also volunteered to send e-mail thank you notes to the pastors of the Rocky Mountain Conference of the United Methodist Church on my behalf. She is always so thoughtful and encouraging to me.

When Fletcher came home, he started packing his clothes in the basement. I asked Fletcher, "At what point did you decide to be kind to Keith?" Fletcher thought about it a little and he replied, "I guess I finally decided to grow up." He said, "Let's get together and have lunch once a week." I asked, "Why? You don't have to worry about me. I have God and I don't need to depend on anyone for emotional support. Why do you want to go out once a week with me?" He answered, "Well, when I needed you the most, you were busy with school. So, I want to practice doing unto others what you would have them do to you." I was thankful for his thoughtfulness. In the kitchen, Fletcher said, "I feel helpless." I asked, "In what way?" He replied, "I cannot bring Dad back. I would bring him back if I could." I saw tears in his eyes. I was choked with tears. Fletcher stood by the koi pond and looked so sad.

I asked Fletcher if he wanted to visit the churches Keith ministered in, and he said no. Fletcher reminded me that I should be careful not to talk about Keith so much because other people will be tired of hearing about my problem. He knew my weaknesses, and I thanked him for his wise advice. He told me to call him anytime if I wanted to talk. I took him to his apartment. I was glad that I was able to spend time with him. "Lord, my children do not have a dad anymore. Please fill their empty hearts with your love and heal their wounds."

## 14. ACDF Friends (7-22-2008)

I visited Lieutenant David Shipley, and he was kind to take time to talk with me. I told him that God has been helping me so much.

*A Story of Hope for Grieving Hearts*                                    29

I was thankful that He was taking care of me. We had a nice talk. He was very thoughtful and compassionate. In 2006, when he heard that I was working on the ACDF inmates' first book, _Maximum Saints Never Hide in the Dark_, he wanted to see me and asked how he could help with the project. He took this project to his church mission board, and Resurrection Fellowship donated $500 for this book project. I was so encouraged. Not only do the ACDF staff and deputies support me, but many inmates from different modules sent me encouraging cards and letters that have touched my heart. I also received many e-mails, cards, and letters from those in the Rocky Mountain and Yellowstone Conferences of the UMC. Many told me that they were praying for my family. I finally threw Keith's shirt and tie in the garbage can after I asked Fletcher if he had seen it, and he said he had. "Lord, I am letting go of some of Keith's belongings. Thank you, Lord, for Keith."

## 15. Thanks (7-23-2008)

A feeling of gratitude is what I feel this morning. All the good things God has given me are His grace. Even in the midst of grieving, he gave me a heart for the incarcerated and homeless. I have been working with a person who will write an article to motivate the Adams County community to start a homeless shelter or transitional house for the homeless inmates released from ACDF. I am praying that the Lord will make it happen through those who have a heart for these poor and suffering people. Even though I wasn't able to work because of my emotional pain, I had peace in my mind. I knew God was with me and helping me. I learned that you can still have peace and joy even in the midst of turmoil and hurting. Paul wrote, _"Rejoice in the Lord always. I will say it again: Rejoice! Let your gentleness be evident to all. The Lord is near. Do not be anxious about anything, but in everything, by prayer and petition, with thanksgiving, present your requests to God. And the peace of God, which transcends all understanding, will guard your hearts and your minds in Christ Jesus."_ (Philippians 4:4-7)

"Lord, bless Keith and help him to be happy beyond his imagination. He was a good husband to me. Thank you, Lord. Please be a Father to my son and my daughter." I remembered what Fletcher said about feeling helpless that he was not able to bring Keith back. That's the feeling I felt when Keith's older brother, Marvin, died in a climbing accident. His family was in shock. I felt bad that they had lost a son, and now they have to go through losing another.

"Lord, please help Keith's parents and bring healing to their hearts. Thank you, Lord, for your grace. You prepared a place for those who believe in you. I am grateful that you remind me of all the good things you have given me in my life, including Keith. You blessed me by calling me to the ministry. You changed my life. My joy and strength comes from you. Keith helped me to realize that not everyone will understand my call in the ministry. In fact, others might misunderstand my motivation and intentions, but you know my heart, Lord. I know you planted the seed of passion to help the incarcerated in my heart. My desire to help the incarcerated does not come from me, but from you. You gave me the heart by helping me to understand their pain and suffering. Many times I am shortsighted and can't see the big picture, so I need your wisdom. At times, I cannot understand Your plans for me. Yet, I trust in you because you proved to me that I can trust you under any circumstance. What more can I say, Lord? You own everything you created, including our souls. You know what I need. I thank you in advance for your grace to let me live in a home that I like: peaceful, beautiful, and gorgeous like a little heavenly home. Thank you for the gift of a house and a little taste of heaven with you."

## 16. TPPM Books (7-24-2008)

Yesterday, Jody, Sara, and Karla came and helped me mail 34 boxes of the *Maximum Saints* and *Journey With Jesus* books to Colorado jails and prisons and to many prisons in other states. Since I wasn't able to work at ACDF, it made me feel good that I was able to send out the books to prisons. "Thank you, Lord."

My friends told me that the Pastor Parish Relationship Committee met with the district superintendent. They were informed that their new pastor would be appointed as early as August 15. I felt rushed to move out since the new pastor might need to stay in the parsonage.

"Lord, it's you. You are the one who will be taking care of me. Thank you, Lord Jesus. Losing Keith is hard, and trying to move out of this place as quickly as possible is really hard. Help me find a house that I like. It's all up to you, Holy Spirit. I need to find a house soon. Please help me." God said, "My daughter, don't worry. I will help you find a house." I asked, "Should I move into a rental home?" God spoke to me, "Keep looking for a house."

## 17. Grieving Together (7-25-2008)

Fletcher and I had lunch and I told him that I was writing an extensive journal of what made me cry, what brought healing in my heart, plus my regular journal. I told him when I thought about how much Keith had suffered, it made me cry. We were both in tears. I also said that I was crying for the loss of our future with Keith. Fletcher said, "I am sad about that, too." Recognizing our loss and talking about our grieving process has helped both of us.

After I looked at more houses, I finally found one that I liked. When I walked into the house, I felt so at home. It had a small, nice backyard, and was beautiful, but the price was higher than what I wanted to pay.

## 18. A House  (7-26-2008)

I looked at more houses, but I still liked the house that I saw yesterday. I made an offer, and it was accepted. The closing date was set for the end of September, so I would be moving out according to my plan. "Thank you, Lord, for your grace."

I work at the hospital as an on-call chaplain once a week, mostly responding to deaths and critical incidents. I went to work at the hospital for the first time since Keith died.

I was helping a woman who lost her husband to cancer. His family which included a 21-year-old daughter and an 18-year-old son stood by the bedside crying. I learned that her family believed in God. She said she had hope of seeing him someday. "But, it will still be difficult," she said. I agreed with her and I mentioned that my husband had passed away 17 days ago. She asked me how I was handling my loss. I told her with lots of tears and by rearranging my thought process, because my husband is not here to make life plans with me anymore. I was glad that there wasn't another death when I was there, because I felt I needed more time to heal my own broken heart.

## 19. River of Tears  (7-27-2008)

I attended James Memorial UMC worship at 9:30 a.m. The interim pastor was there and gave me a warm welcome. I thanked the congregation for their support in my grieving process. I went to attend Community UMC, and when the congregation started singing a hymn, the reality of Keith's death hit me hard. I tried to stop my tears, but I couldn't. Keith would have been there leading worship if he were alive, but he can't do that anymore. I finally got up and told Jody that I couldn't stay for worship because I couldn't stop my tears. I asked her to tell the congregation how thankful I am for their prayers and support.

When I got home, for the first time I asked, "Why? Why are you letting me go through this? Why did you choose me to go through this?" When I got tired of crying, I decided to go to ACDF and visit

Deputy Duran. When I called the operator at the facility, the deputy who answered the phone recognized my voice and talked to me for quite a while to comfort me. She told me to watch funny movies and that would help my grieving process. I visited Deputy Duran and we had a good talk. She is always encouraging me, and that brings healing in my heart.

Nicole sent me an e-mail which made me cry. I knew she would miss her dad. She mentioned that what she will miss is conversations with Keith about different issues. If she wanted to ask Keith a question, she wouldn't be able to anymore. She wondered how I was doing and asked me if I was able to go back to work. While I was responding to her, I couldn't stop crying. Nicole was hurting, but I couldn't help her because of my own pain.

I started writing outlines for a book on grieving and healing. For a long time, I had planned to write a book on how to experience healing from grief and loss. As a chaplain, I help many people deal with death and dying. I thought it would be nice to have a book. Then, when someone lost a loved one, I could hand them a book so they could get help. I have been busy with other writing projects though and I had no idea how I would go about writing on the subject of grieving.

Keith was an excellent writer. He told me he wanted to make a devotional book with his parish and his friends' stories. He hadn't received any response from them. After he passed away, people were asking me if I was going to make Keith's book. I tried to gather his email devotion from his computer files. I only found two devotions. I asked the Lord if I should write the book about grief and healing. He replied, "My daughter, I have planned it. Go for it. I will lead you to help more people through the pain, suffering, and grieving." I said, "Thank you Lord. I feel this is going to be my grief book instead of Keith's devotional book." God replied, "This book is going to help many people who are grieving, so it has to be your book."

Since Keith died, today is the first day I thought about helping Nicole and Fletcher with their grieving process. I asked my mother-in-law and father-in-law to take Keith's ashes to bury next to Marvin in Spokane, Washington, next year. Keith's parents told me that they already paid for a burial site. They also said they have two extra spots, so if anyone in our family wanted to use them they could. I always wanted to be buried next to Keith, so I thought it might work out. I started thinking that Spokane might be too far for Nicole and myself. I thought if we bury Keith's ashes in Buffalo, Nicole wouldn't have to travel so far and I could visit Keith's grave often. I thought about making a tombstone for Keith and myself, since I could be buried next to him someday. I knew I needed to discuss this with my children to find out what would be best for all of us.

I started cleaning Keith's study and packing his books. The whole time I was packing his books and labeling them, I couldn't stop my tears. It took me two full days because he had so many books. All the memories rushed back to me since Keith kept all of his books. I have many good memories of Multnomah Bible College because we attended there together. Again, I reminded myself that it was God's grace that I was able to clean his study for the last time.

I was going to donate Keith's books, but Nicole told me she would like to go through all the books to find out which ones she wanted to keep. I sent 35 boxes of books to her. I realized that she needed time to grieve, and that going through Keith's books would help her.

I reflected on what happened before Keith's accident. It is still puzzling to me. Something was missing: either Keith's ability to make a sound judgment at the time he was driving or the busy intersection with no lights and poor visibility caused him not to see the on-coming car. About a month or two before Keith's accident, I had a strange experience at the crossroad where he had the accident. I was driving alone at the time. As I approached the crossroad, suddenly a thought came to me and I slowed down. If someone suddenly turned left, I knew I would not have enough time to stop in a 65-mile-per-hour zone. It was just too busy and had no signal lights. Why had I asked that question at that intersection? I have no idea. As far as I can remember, I've never had any experience like that in any other place.

In addition, about three or four months before Keith's accident, he shared that Brighton police officers had stopped him three times for traffic violations within a month. He said he even got a warning ticket because he did not signal to change lanes. One day, he got a ticket in Brighton when I was in the car. He was making a right turn, but he failed to see the 'No Turn On Red' sign. I thought it was strange that Keith had gotten so many tickets in a short period of time, since Keith had always been a careful driver. Only the Lord knows what happened, and I am still puzzled about how Keith could have not seen the on-coming car.

## 20. Not Ready  (7-28-2008)
It's been twenty days since Keith passed away. In the midst of all of the emotional ups and downs, I wasn't sure if I was ready to lead

the worship service at ACDF. I decided to try, so I asked Pastor Daniel to come and help me in case I needed him. Daniel has filled in for me when I was gone. After I took care of some urgent messages on the phone and visited inmates, I went to lead the worship service with Pastor Daniel in the C Module.

As Daniel was gathering inmates for worship, some came up to me and said that they were sorry about what happened to my husband. They had been praying for me. I thanked them. As the contact room filled with more inmates, I could feel the air getting thick. It was so thick. I've never felt anything like it. I knew from the look of the inmates that they were wondering how I was handling my grief and loss. We began with a song. I usually led a prayer after that. I love to lead prayers because the Holy Spirit can use the prayer time to speak to people and bring healing. For the first time in my life, I was emotionally immobilized from grief and sorrow, I couldn't lead prayer. I couldn't say a word of thanks to the people sitting and looking at me with care and deep concern. I asked Daniel to lead worship, and I left. I needed more healing before I could go back to work at ACDF.

As I was leaving the facility, I was in tears. I did not want to go to an empty home. I called Fletcher and asked him if he wanted to go out to dinner, and he said yes. I took him to a Korean restaurant. We talked about Keith and I knew our sharing and reflection would bring continuous healing. After dinner, I bought two pounds of Bulgogi, which is marinated beef, for him because he likes it. Fletcher looked so happy and thanked me. Then he said, "Do you know that you are spoiling me?" I replied, "I am doing it intentionally. Do you know why I try to help you?" He asked, "Why?" I said, "Two reasons. One is people who receive can learn to give generously to others. People who do not receive have a hard time being generous to others. My mother taught me how to give. She gave me $1,000 when I started attending The Iliff School of Theology. That was a lot of money for her, but she did it to encourage me. My mother was so proud of me because I made a decision to go into ministry. She helped me with room and board while I was attending school. I didn't have any money to help her. Because of her generosity, I learned to give. Second, I don't want you to be in survival mode. People who are in survival mode lack the vision to help others. Survival mode sometimes hinders our aspirations and dreams because we are desperately focusing on meeting our own basic needs. I want you to go beyond your own needs and help others. Do you know anyone who struggles financially and sends their children on a mission trip which costs a lot?" He said, "I don't know any, but you did it." I replied, "I did it because I wanted you to have a bigger vision for your life. To be happy and have a fulfilled life is to follow our dreams, visions, and aspirations to help others."

When I explained to Fletcher what kind of house I was planning to buy, he liked the idea, even though he hadn't seen it. I also mentioned that I wanted to bury Keith's ashes in Buffalo so our family will be close to Keith's grave. Fletcher told me he did not have a good memory of Buffalo. He also mentioned that Keith told him that he did not want to be buried, but would like his ashes sprinkled at Flathead Lake in Kalispell, Montana. Our family fished there and we had a great time at the camp when our kids were little.

About a month before Keith died, we were discussing where we would be buried. He told me he did not want to be buried, and I took it as a joke. I always wanted to be buried next to him, so his words did not sink in at the time. Fletcher's words reminded me of what he had said. In addition, Karla called me and told me that Keith told his youth group that when he died he didn't want to be buried, but wanted his ashes spread at Flathead Lake. Keith and I had made our wills, and I knew he wanted to be cremated. He did not say where he wanted his ashes spread. My desire to be buried next to him was gone forever. After these conversations, I called Keith's parents and told them that we would be spreading Keith's ashes at Flathead Lake when we get together in 2009.

## 21. Triggers  (7-29-2008)

Even though God had been helping me through Scripture and bringing healing in some areas, I was still at the point of breaking down whenever I was reminded of Keith. I was learning about my triggers. Everyday life, and almost anything or anyone, could be a trigger. Dishes and silverware he bought were a trigger. If I saw someone who looked like Keith, I was sad that he wasn't here anymore. If I saw a red truck on the street, I was again reminded of how Keith died. When I saw a couple walking together, it reminded me of the good old days when we went for walks in the park. It made me sad. If I saw something beautiful, I was sad that I could not share it with Keith.

Driving was another trigger. My thoughts were always focused on what happened to him on the road. I was deeply immersed on a path of grief and pain. I did not realize how much Keith meant to me. I was always making plans with him for the future. I can't do that anymore. All my expectations in life, all my desires, all my future plans, dreams, and wishes were related to Keith. I just didn't know how to handle

*Dancing in the Sky*

these triggers. This was something new to me. I was in constant turmoil, I could break down any time. I couldn't control my tears.

I started making plans to celebrate Keith's life after I moved into the new house. I thought about honoring him by planting a memorial tree in the backyard. I made plans to make a special corner to celebrate his life in my new home. I had no desire to let him go. Since I knew that Keith could not be a part of my life anymore, I wanted to hang on to what I could.

At this point, I had no idea how I could experience healing from these triggers. I thought holding on to Keith would help me in my healing. Everything Keith had spent time to build became precious to me. I was looking at the koi pond and thought about how much time and energy Keith had spent building it. I wanted to take the pond to my new home, if I could. I was attached to everything that we enjoyed together. In reality, the koi pond wouldn't look good in my new home, and my back yard does not have enough room. My grieving consumed so much of my time and energy that I was not able to work on my writing project. It also hindered my prayer time with the Lord. I just did not know how to heal at this point.

22. His Clothes (7-30-2008)

I started going through Keith's clothes, and I was crying the whole time. Jeaneane wanted some that have United Methodist symbols or Tae Kwon Do logos on them to make quilts to remember Keith. I started asking, "Why, Lord, did you choose me to go through this? What are you trying to teach me through this?" God spoke to my heart, "My daughter, my grace is sufficient in all circumstances. You will learn that again and again in the worst situations. I will teach you many things through this loss, and I will bless you through this." I said, "Thank you, God. Your grace is sufficient for me."

I packed two big boxes for Jeaneane and mailed them to her. I sent the rest of the clothes to a thrift shop. I called Jeaneane and asked how she was doing. She told me Keith's death was affecting her, and it was not easy. I thanked her for the book on grieving because it had many good suggestions. She said she felt she needed to go and buy a book on grief for herself. She did not sound good, and she definitely needed help. Keith's death shook so many people.

I was grateful God was allowing me to buy a house that I liked. I asked the Lord, "Why, Lord? You blessed me so much with the house that I am going to buy. I feel I don't deserve it." The Lord said, "I want you to taste a little bit of heaven." I am glad that God is allowing me to experience heaven before I get there. I prayed, "Lord, bless my new home so everyone who walks into my house will experience the presence of the Lord and your beauty."

### 23. Two Malamutes  (8-1-2008)

Since I wasn't ready to go back to work, Fletcher and I drove to Buffalo to visit Nicole's family. Nicole took Keith's two dogs, Bradley and Jaffa. She was busy taking care of her three little kids, two kittens, and the two dogs. Nicole said she was going to put a fence around the house so the dogs could run around. I understood that Nicole became attached to the dogs because they were Keith's, but I knew it was too much work for her. Fletcher took Jaffa for a walk, and I thought he was kind to do that. That's what Keith would be doing if he were there.

### 24. Good-Byes  (8-2-2008)

I enjoy spending time with my three granddaughters: Teila, the four-year-old, Jamie, two-years-old, and Lindsay the youngest. Sleeping in my arms that morning Lindsay looked so peaceful and beautiful. I was reading the accident report. The picture in the report showed how Keith's car rolled, which made me cry. I saw the word expired on the following page next to Keith's name. Keith was expired. I heard that term many times at the hospital when someone passed away. It had never made me cry, but this time it did.

Nicole took Lindsay and walked out of the house to go to the hospital for an appointment. Teila was desperately trying to catch up with her mom. She said, "Bye, Mom," but Nicole drove off. Teila looked so sad and was almost in tears as she walked around the living room. I stopped her and asked how she was doing. She said, "I feel sad. I couldn't say bye to my Mom." I gave her a hug and said, "She will be home soon. She had to take Lindsay to the hospital."

After I went into the room I started reflecting on what Teila said. Then, I realized that I, too, was not able to say good-bye to Keith. I was crying. Then God reminded me of the dream I had after Keith died. He came, bowed to me, and said, "Thank you." I heard his voice and he disappeared. I believe that was his way of saying good-bye to me. I heard his voice so clearly. That was a blessing. God's word, "My grace is sufficient for you,", is truly right. "Thank you, Jesus. Even though I couldn't say bye to Keith, you let him say bye to me." I missed Keith.

Our grandchildren will not be able to spend time with him anymore. Keith loved our grandkids, and whenever we visited he took

*Dancing in the Sky*

wonderful family photos and showed them to everyone. There was no one taking pictures this time. No one can replace him. I did not realize how much joy he had brought until he was gone. I took everything, even his humor, for granted. "Thank you, Lord Jesus, for your grace and that you are taking care of him. I need your grace and wisdom to love you and serve you better."

I took a nap and had a dream. I don't know how, but Keith was close by me even though he couldn't talk to me or reveal himself to me. I saw him, but I couldn't touch him. He was wearing a white and yellow sweatshirt which he wore when our kids were little. When I woke up, God said, "My daughter, I'm taking care of Keith. You should not worry."

This dream reminded me of the story of a Korean pastor who had a stroke and was dead for four hours. Two angels took his spirit to show him heaven and hell. In heaven, Jesus told him to tell the world that there is a heaven and hell and to preach the gospel. After the angels gave the tour of heaven and hell, he was leaving to go back to his earthly life. His deceased mother appeared to him and told him that she saw her son suffering. She had been praying for his healing, so he could preach again. God answered her prayers. After the pastor came back to life, he wrote a book about his experience. He received many invitations to preach. Jesus gave him an assignment to build a retirement home for 50 retired pastors who did not have children to take care of them. With the money he received from the book and his preaching, he bought the land to build a retirement home. His story teaches me that people who die, especially those who are with the Lord, know how their loved ones are doing and pray for them. Jesus prays for us, and I believe Keith is praying for his family as well.

I had a talk with Fletcher about how people would look in heaven. We even joked around that if everyone looked younger, Keith would have more hair on his head. Keith had lost a lot of hair in his older age, but he had a lot of hair when our kids were little.

I had a dream that I was driving with Keith. I stepped out of the car to talk to someone, then Keith drove off. When I called him on the phone, he said, "Didn't I tell you that I should be at The Iliff School of Theology by 5:00 p.m.?" I was upset that he did not wait for me. I told him I would get a ride to find him. After I woke up, I thought God was trying to tell me that I needed to separate from my emotional attachment to Keith to deal with my life constructively. Memories serve a good purpose, but when I am consumed with the past, I cannot live fully in the present and cannot function normally. I cannot have visions, cannot dream, I don't have time to think about others' pain or understand what needs to be done to help them. When I am in pain, it's hard to love God with my whole heart, mind, soul, and strength. My grieving was hindering my relationship with the Lord. I had to release Keith, so I prayed.

"Lord, I am learning that I need to treat Keith as one of the other deceased and resurrected saints in Christ, and not as my husband anymore. I ask you to take away my obsession for him. Please help me to let go of Keith. I cannot be consumed with thoughts of him, but that is what is happening. I give him to you who created us both. I know this is the only way I can experience healing."

# Chapter Two: Triggers of Pain & Gifts of Healing

## 1. Dancing in the Sky (8-3-2008)

Today Fletcher and I left Buffalo and drove back to Denver. We went to a Vietnamese restaurant and enjoyed dinner. Fletcher asked me if I truly loved Keith. I had to think for a moment. I couldn't believe he would ask a question like that. I replied, "Yes. I loved Keith more than anyone else I have ever met. I have to be honest with my feelings. If I didn't love him, I would not have stayed married. You will understand later. You cannot live with a person that long if you don't love them. Even though we had struggles and challenges, we loved each other and that kept our family together. We were always faithful to each other. There was no doubt in my mind that he loved me. One of our friends divorced his wife, and I asked him what the reason was for the break up. He said to me that he did not love his wife. He said he just couldn't be with her in the same house. He tried so hard to love her, but he couldn't. He wasn't happy being around her and finally he concluded that divorce was the only option. He told me he was happier after he divorced his wife. I was happy around Keith, and he was upset when I wasn't around much." Fletcher said, "I just wanted to know."

After I took Fletcher to his apartment, I was driving alone, listening to "God of Wonders," one of Keith's favorite songs. I was at 1-76 and Hwy 85, not far from Brighton, and suddenly I saw a vision of Keith dancing in the sky. He was wearing a yellow shirt, brown shorts, and tennis shoes. He started on my right side, then circled around and was dancing on my left. He was dancing so well. I saw his happy smile. I couldn't believe my eyes. I was almost in tears, filled with so much joy and excitement. God is truly alive and has comforted me through this vision. Keith was truly happy in the presence of God in heaven. This vision lasted for a while and then disappeared.

About ten years ago, when I woke up, God said, "You and I will talk about wonders." I had no idea what "wonders" meant at the time, and I still don't. But, I am beginning to realize that when God teaches us what wonders are, they go beyond our imagination. I never guessed that God would show me Keith dancing in the sky.

When Keith was alive, I wanted to learn how to dance with him, so I suggested we join a dance club. He told me he couldn't dance. I had no interest in dancing with anyone but him, so I gave up that idea. It was God's grace that He allowed me to have a vision of Keith dancing with a happy smile. I can tell the world that God is real and can bring healing to grieving hearts. The message was clear from this vision. Keith was happy in heaven. I, too, should be happy instead of continuously grieving.

This vision of Keith dancing made me so happy. The spiritual world is real and encouraging. Keith is truly enjoying his life with God in heaven. I rejoiced knowing that Keith finally lives in paradise with Jesus. "Thank you, Lord, for your grace for letting me know that Keith is doing well and is happy in heaven."

## 2. Taste of Heaven (8-4-2008)

God brought me so much healing through the vision of Keith dancing. I was able to go back to work at ACDF the next morning. God performed a miracle. A week ago, I walked out of C Module worship in tears, not knowing when I could go back to work. This time, I had the courage to share my journey of grief. God brought healing in my heart through words, dreams, and a vision. I was thankful to share the power of God through my testimony in C Module. After I shared my testimony, one inmate leader preached, and I felt the warmth of the Holy Spirit's healing power flowing and spreading out through this man. It touched my heart and filled me with joy. God is powerful and compassionate. The Holy Spirit's healing presence was real.

I was blessed. I questioned, "Would I be able to help others with the power of the Holy Spirit and bring healing like that?" I prayed, "Lord, anoint me so others will be blessed through my ministry. Thank you, Lord." God blessed me with these words from Proverbs: *"Trust in the Lord with all your heart and lean not on your own understanding; in all your ways acknowledge him, and he will make your paths straight." (Proverbs 3:5-6)* This is the Scripture I preached the first week I went back to ACDF.

On July 10, Timothy Garcia, from A3, was going to be a part of a DVD project to help youth.· I had to cancel because of my husband's death. When I was leading worship in A3, an inmate asked me if the devil had caused my husband's accident to discourage my ministry. I told him that Jesus said not one of His sparrows will fall to the ground without God's will. (Matthew 10:29) I don't give the devil credit or even question if the devil was the cause of the accident. God doesn't want people to die a tragic death, but accidents happen and people die. It's a part of life. If Keith were supposed to live longer, he would have survived the accident. I shared that God helped me accept my husband's death by letting me understand that my husband lived a full

*Dancing in the Sky*

life. Many who came to worship were encouraged because of my testimony. Some said that my coming back to the facility and to continue work for the Lord shows that He is real.

I remembered what God had said, "You will have a little taste of heaven." Somehow this new house that I bought may be what God was referring to, since I felt beauty when I walked into the house. Also, I believe the vision of Keith dancing in the sky was a little taste of heaven.

### 3. Frog Eyes (8-5-2008)

In a dream, I saw Keith peeking at me and making his eyes look like frog eyes, as if he was trying to make me laugh. He occasionally did when he was alive. I laughed loudly, then woke up. I thanked God for making me laugh through Keith's humor. The message was that Keith was doing fine, and I should not be grieving. It's good to remember him, but not to be immersed in deep sadness or pain. But it seems letting go of Keith and not grieving because he is in heaven was only a concept to me even though I said I believed. I still did not know how to let go of him. I thought holding on to him was honoring him.

### 4. My Wish (8-9-2008)

Today is one month since Keith's death. While I was leading a song, God said, "You have lost someone you loved the most." I was in tears because it was true. Then, He spoke to me, "I will bring healing in your heart." I didn't know how, but I was thankful that God was going to heal my broken heart.

At the hospital, I was called to the Emergency Room for a dying man. He was breathing with the help of a machine. He was 67 years old and there was no family present. He was living with a man who did not have any plans to be at the hospital, even after he heard that his friend was dying.

I thought about my husband's last moments at the hospital. Keith was already dead when they found him. He lasted a little longer because of CPR and the chemicals that were pumped into his body. I could see in my mind what they did to Keith. I have seen it too many times in the Emergency Room while the hospital staff tries to revive the person. I have watched people die and have seen how devastating it is for the family.

I would have been with Keith if I had known what was happening. "I am sorry that you had to die alone, Keith," I couldn't help but cry. It was good that there were no other critical incidents that night.

I was hurting badly inside and it would have been difficult for me to minister to anyone. "Thank you, God, for taking care of Keith."

## 5. Joy of Giving  (8-10-2008)

I was on my way to a retreat in Santa Fe. On the way to the airport I met Glenn at the post office. He was from Community UMC and is one of the most gentlest, kindest, and generous person I've ever met. He told me he wanted to give me a gift and gave me $20. He mentioned how much Keith and I helped the community. He was in tears, and that brought me to tears. I thanked him, and told him I would give it to the Transformation Project since he had donated to the book project earlier. He said that it was for me.

When I arrived in Santa Fe, I took a bus to the Immaculate Heart of Mary where the National Association of United Methodist Korean-American Women Clergy was having a retreat. The Holy Spirit told me to give the driver $20 for lunch. The man was so appreciative of it. Glenn was happy that he was able to give me the gift. I was happy that I received the gift. I was happy because I was able to give the gift to the bus driver. The bus driver was happy because he received an unexpected gift. The giver always receives more than the recipient. God gave me joy by obeying Him. God teaches us about the joy of giving. He can do so much with just $20 when we obey the Lord.

I received much encouragement and support from other clergy women. I was glad that I went to this retreat. At first, I almost cancelled because I was still grieving, but I always enjoyed the Korean Women's Clergy retreat. In fact, this is one of the most inspirational retreats of the year. This gathering has brought so much healing and joy to my heart.

## 6. The Flowers  (8-11-2008)

Our retreat started with worshiping the Lord in the beautiful chapel. When we were singing "I Love You Lord," I felt the Holy Spirit's anointing and that brought tears to my eyes. The Korean-American Women Clergy retreat is always so uplifting and the Holy Spirit's presence is strong because many have paid the price for following the Lord with courage and boldness.

As I was walking out of the chapel, I saw beautiful flowers. I thought about how much Keith is enjoying flowers and fish in heaven. Keith can enjoy fish without worrying about freezing them to death. The thought that Keith is in a better place brought joy to my heart. I realized that I should not focus on what I had lost, but what Keith had gained. Death is a loss for those who are grieving, but is a gain for those who know the Lord.

### 7. Laughter and Healing  (8-12-2008)

Today we went on a tour, and the best part was the time we spent on the bus. We all shared our spiritual journeys and sang. I had a great time because many women pastors have a great sense of humor, and the laughter helped me. "Thank you, Lord. This is one of the best retreats I've ever attended." Laughter brought healing. For awhile I forgot about my pain. I needed to take a break from my grieving and tears.

### 8. Proud of Him  (8-13-2008)

In the middle of the retreat, during one of the sessions, I went back to my room and spent time in prayer. I was grieving. I prayed to God to help Keith recognize my love for him. I prayed for my children, my family, and others who needed healing from grief.

At this retreat I learned something new. I used to talk about my husband and join their conversations and laugh along with them. This time, it was different. When other women talked about their husbands, it was as if someone hurt my wounds. I felt sad and was in tears.

I thought I was strong. I did not rely on my husband for my self -identity, and I still don't. I've already developed my own identity, and I am happy with myself. I am emotionally independent from Keith. Still, just listening to others tell about how their husbands were good to them made me realize what I had lost.

I was vulnerable and everything reminded me of the loss of Keith. I knew I needed to get over this feeling of self-pity, but I didn't know how. Obviously, Keith gave me more emotional support than I realized. For a long time, I had someone that I loved and trusted, but now he is gone. I just did not know how proud I was of Keith.

Paul tells us to *"Rejoice with those who rejoice; mourn with those who mourn." (Romans 12:15)* I was in so much pain and grief that I was not able to rejoice with those who rejoice.

"Lord Jesus, give me the wisdom to handle this. Help me to have the grace to hear and listen to others' relationships without being sad. Help me to get over this self-pity. Thank you, Lord."

### 9. Prayer and Pain  (8-14-2008)

I began to realize more and more how much Keith was a big part of my life. His presence at home was a gift. He spent more time at home than I did since his office was there. Even though we had different hobbies and interests, Keith was good at making me participate in his hobbies, which I appreciated. I know I cannot find anyone to replace him. I am mourning the loss of a close friend.

"Lord, I give you my pain. Please heal my grieving heart. No one can heal my wounds but you. Thank you for your healing power."

## 10. Music and Healing (8-15-2008)

I was glad that I made it to the retreat. I learned that a different environment and meeting different people can bring healing to my mind and heart. Thank you, Lord, for everyone who showed concern and love. At the retreat, I received a CD of harmonica music. I was blessed. It was like a little taste of heaven. Music brings healing.

"Lord, anoint me so people who come to chaplain's worship can have a little taste of heaven." I was reading the book of Jeremiah, and it touched me. *"No one is like you, O Lord; you are great, and your name is mighty in power. Who should not revere you, O King of the nations? This is your due. Among all the wise men of the nations and in all their kingdoms, there is no one like you." (Jeremiah 10:6-7)*

Jeremiah 9:23-24 says, *"'Let not the wise man boast of his wisdom or the strong man boast of his strength or the rich man boast of his riches, but let him who boasts boast about this: that he understands and knows me, that I am the Lord, who exercises kindness, justice and righteousness on earth, for in these I delight,' declares the Lord."*

## 11. Prison Ministry (8-16-2008)

I called my older brother in Korea for the first time since I lost my husband. I had no heart to talk to him before, but about a week ago I sent an e-mail to my niece to let her family know that Keith had passed away. My brother immediately called me and left a message to call him back. I had no desire to talk to him. When he had lost his son early in 2008 from suicide, I visited him and his family. They were devastated by their loss. My brother came out to the airport before I left Korea. While I was waiting at the airport, my brother told me that since his son died he had no desire to live. He was hurting badly.

While on the phone talking about Keith's passing, I was trying to share how God was helping me in my grieving process. I told my brother that I have faith in God and hope to see Keith in heaven someday. He said, "Oh, there is no heaven." I replied, "I believe there is God and heaven and hell." This conversation made me sad. My mother has been praying for my brother's salvation all of her life.

After I graduated from The Iliff School of Theology, one of the places for which I interviewed was the Denver Rescue Mission chaplaincy. In the process of interviewing, God helped me to have the heart to invite my brother to the states. I was concerned about our finances. Then God gave me a dream about how much my older brother had been suffering at the hand of the devil, but that he eventually would be freed from pain. I was so encouraged by that dream that I started the paperwork to invite him to the United States.

In those days, when God reminded me of my brother's hardships I shed many tears. My brother has a special place in my heart. I know how much he suffered under our abusive, alcoholic father. My father hated my brother, and he abused him physically, mentally, and emotionally. When my father started beating my mother, my brother couldn't handle watching it. He ran away from home and was homeless at the age of eleven, got involved with gangs and was incarcerated three times. Our family suffered a lot from our father's abusive behavior until he committed suicide in 1978, one-and-a-half months after I got married. He was drunk when he killed himself.

In the summer of 1999, before I started attending The Iliff School of Theology, I asked the Lord what kind of ministry He wanted me to do. I felt my ministry was not inside the church. The next day God reminded me of the second visit I made to my brother when he was incarcerated in Korea. I felt that if we had had a loving home he would not have run away and would not have gotten into trouble with the law. I was so overwhelmed with sorrow and grief that I was crying in the waiting room. I tried to stop crying, but I just couldn't.

My brother and I were very close. He cared deeply about me. He was my protector and security on the streets. When they called me to see my brother, I was still crying. When my brother saw me he said, "Why did you come?" Unable to answer, I walked out of the place in tears. I never went back to see him because it hurt me to see him in prison.

When God reminded me of this visit, He also reminded me of what I wanted to see in my older brother's incarceration. I wanted to see only one thing. I wanted someone to introduce Jesus to my brother so he could be saved, find hope, and direction. It never happened. What I wanted other people to do for my brother, God was asking me to do. He spoke to my heart, "Go and tell them that they are forgiven. Treat them as if they are your older brother."

I did not know prison ministry even existed until God spoke to me. It was incredible to watch how God works in prisons. If I would have known that earlier, I would have gone into the ministry.

## 12. Father Phil Negele (8-17-2008)

Father Phil is a Catholic priest and a hospital chaplain where I work. He is in his 80s and is more like my spiritual mentor. If I have a difficult question, I ask him. He also has been my source of encouragement, and I have shared with him the Transformation Project.

One day he cut out an article about how many Harry Potter books were sold. He told me I have to make sure that TPPM should try to distribute more books than Harry Potter did. I told him it was great that he was challenging me to do better.

Father Phil told me one day that he would vote for me for president. I told him I wasn't even born in America and asked, "Why do you want to vote for me for a president?" He replied, "I've never seen anyone who can accomplish more than you."

After I learned that he was hospitalized and was in the Intensive Care Unit (ICU), I visited him. He was in good spirits. It was good to see his smile. I was concerned about him. I was still grieving and I didn't think I could handle any more losses. I thanked God that he was doing well.

## 13. Anointing (8-18-2008)

God is teaching me how to win spiritual battles through David's Psalm 23. I especially like verses 5 and 6. When we are hurting, that is the time the devil tries to turn us away from the Lord, as if God caused the pain and suffering. We can praise and worship the Lord no matter what happens.

I shared in chaplain's worship services that when we are tempted, we can recite Psalm 23:5: *"You prepare a table before me in the presence of my enemies. You anoint my head with oil; my cup overflows."* I am learning that in grieving, I can worship God and thank Him for his blessings. The devil doesn't have power when we start praising God. I was so obsessed with the loss of Keith that I forgot about God's blessings. God encouraged me through that Scripture. I need to focus on God's grace, so I can experience healing in my life.

## 14. Driving (8-19-2008)

The first 40 days after Keith died, I was busy taking care of his paperwork, closing all of his accounts, and taking care of his belongings. I had so much to pack, to go through, and to decide what to keep. All of these processes became triggers of grief.

I was beginning to understand what other grieving spouses were going through more and more through my triggers. Grieving for Keith was hard and sometimes dangerous, because grieving distorted my decision making process. My thoughts were always focused on how I lost Keith and how much I missed him. I had so many memories, and my thought process had to be adjusted. Because God was helping me, I was functioning much better at work and was able to minister.

The major break came after God gave me the vision of Keith dancing in the sky, but still my grieving process was not done. I still had to take care of all of the areas that were triggers and reminded me of the loss. My emotions were up and down every day. I knew I had to go through many tears. I knew I had no choice at that point, because I did not know any better. There were a lot of lessons to learn through this painful process.

One area in which I was affected by grief was driving, because he died on the road. I couldn't believe how full my mind was with the thoughts of what happened the day he died. Whenever I was driving, it was almost like I was entering a grief zone. My mind played his accident scene over and over. I couldn't stop playing it. All I could do was try to be very careful driving, because my mind was full of Keith. One day, I had a dream that I was stopped by a police officer. I was trying to give him an excuse of why and how I made a mistake.

On my way to pick up Fletcher, I was crying. I was thinking about the intense pain Keith had felt when his car rolled over and landed on him. I told myself I shouldn't be crying because my eyes would get red, and Fletcher will notice. I did not want him to worry. I just couldn't stop crying. I stopped in front of a left turn signal. I was waiting for the light to turn green. The place where Keith had his accident did not have signal lights. I saw an on-coming car, and without thinking, I turned left and barely missed it. I couldn't believe what I did. It could have been fatal if I had been hit by the car. My children don't need to lose their mom in a car accident like they lost their dad.

I was in shock as I began to realize how grief can affect my abilities and decision-making process. I did not tell Fletcher about my mistake that day. He was already concerned about how I was dealing with the loss. I believe that is one of the reasons why he suggested that we should get together once a week to have dinner.

## 15. An Invitation to Pray (8-20-2008)

While living in Glasgow, Montana, God called me to pray for ten percent of my time when I was resisting my call to ministry. I started praying more, and then God spoke to me to pray five hours a day. It was difficult to do that, so I forgot about it. Then this morning, for the second time, God asked me to pray five hours daily. Because of this request, I decided to simplify my life as much as possible, so I would be able to spend more time with the Lord.

I prayed, "How can I spend five hours with you, Lord? Holy Spirit, I need your help." I know it's difficult, but if the Holy Spirit can help me, I believe it's possible. "Lord Jesus, let my love bloom in your garden like a rose. Let my love for you bloom and bring a smile to your face."

Today, I remembered to write a weekly devotion for "Reflections" for the Upper Room. "Reflections" is a daily devotion for 365 days. The study is based on the three-year lectionary Bible reading. My story will be coming out in 2010. I need to finish it in time to send it to the Upper Room publisher. I decided to add a story of how God is helping me with my grieving process.

I was reading Scripture and Psalm 31:7-10, which made me cry. It says, *"I will be glad and rejoice in your love, for you saw my affliction and knew the anguish of my soul. You have not handed me over to the enemy but have set my feet in a spacious place. Be merciful to me, O Lord, for I am in distress; my eyes grow weak with sorrow, my soul and my body with grief. My life is consumed by anguish and my years by groaning; my strength fails because of my affliction, and my bones grow weak."*

I am thankful that God can heal my broken heart. Also, my friends brought healing because of their kindness. Martha brought me breakfast burritos and helped me pack. Jody also came and helped me pack and took more boxes to the dump and the thrift shop.

## 16. Encouragement (8-21-2008)

I have one regret. I wish I had let Keith know how proud I was. I wrote two letters to encourage Keith in our 30 years of marriage. The first one was after we moved to Glasgow. God healed me from my backsliding and helped me to recognize how much Keith made a difference in my life and others' lives. After we moved to Keenesburg, God asked me to write about all the good things Keith had done since the beginning of our marriage. I wrote a letter in 2007. God brought healing in my heart while I was writing it. Keith was very happy when I gave him the letter. I asked God for forgiveness because I should have been more encouraging to Keith. He had good intentions and worked hard for the Lord.

I received a veteran's paper about tombstones. I was overwhelmed with sorrow as I was looking at it. I was also looking at Keith's pictures. That made me cry. I missed him. "God, help me not to grieve, but to celebrate his final graduation with the honor."

The same day, I received a wooden cross with the United Methodist Church logo on it from Rocky Mountain Conference. I was happy to receive it because I am a United Methodist minister and that logo is special to me.

## 17. Desert Mothers and Fathers (8-22-2008)

I started wondering again how I could spend five hours with the Lord. I thought it would help to spend time with the Lord as soon as I woke up and before I went to bed. Also, I decided to simplify my lifestyle and to eliminate distraction from emotional involvements and attachments. I asked God for the wisdom to deal with these and let them go. I learned that even having pets is a hindrance for me.

I remembered stories of desert mothers and fathers in the early centuries, who decided to spend more time with the Lord. They went to the desert where there was no one, so they could devote their time to the Lord. God has prepared a perfect environment for me where I hardly have to worry about anything, just focusing on prayer and ministering. It's God's grace that He is asking me to spend more time with Him.

## 18. Proving Love (8-23-2008)

God asked me, "If you love someone so much, wouldn't you love to spend five hours with that person?" I answered, "Yes Lord, I love you. You know I love you. Didn't I prove it when I decided to go into the ministry? Didn't I prove it when I decided to commute 430 miles to attend seminary for three years? I almost died in a car accident, but I kept going because I felt your calling. Lord Jesus, I love you. Let my love for you blossom in your garden and bring a smile to your face. Lord, thank you for everything. Help me so I can spend more time with you."

## 19. The Birthday Card (8-24-2008)

In Keith's study, I found the last birthday card he had bought for Fletcher. He did not sign it, but I gave it to my son. I couldn't help being choked with tears. When I was checking Fletcher's box, I saw the card. I prayed, "Lord, help Fletcher to know how much Keith loved and cared for him. Keith was very proud of him." I knew Keith deeply cared for Fletcher. The card said, "For a terrific son." "Thank you Lord

Jesus, for Keith's love for his family."

### 20. Grace  (8-25-2008)
Today, I realized how many blessings I have received from the Lord. One of them was being married to Keith, but I took it for granted. I lived as if Keith would always be there for me and for our family. "Lord, it was your grace that you took care of me through my husband. My healing came through Keith in many ways. He blessed me more than anyone else I have ever met. It's because of his love and kindness that I have many wonderful memories of him. Help me to be aware of the blessings you have showered on me so I don't take anything for granted."

### 21. My Book Project  (8-26-2008)
My friend Julia is translating *Journey With Jesus* and *Maximum Saints Ordained by God* into Spanish for the Hispanic inmates. I am really excited about this project because the books will be going to many jails and prisons to help the incarcerated find God and grow in faith. However, I stopped the book project completely after Keith died. I am in so much pain that just making the arrangements for editing the Spanish book was too much for me.  I cannot concentrate on any book project. I have to wait until I can handle it.

### 22. The Little Cat, Joan  (8-27-2008)
While Keith was alive, he took care of all of his pets, but I knew I couldn't take care of them. I decided to let all the pets go, including my two fish.
I was glad that a family took all the pigeons, as well as the loft, hauling it away with a big trailer. I gave my two fish to a deputy at ACDF.  Nicole was trying to take care of Keith's two dogs, but she was busy taking care of her three kids and her four pets. I learned that Karla's daughter, Sue Ann, always wanted to have big dogs and wanted to have Bradley and Jaffa.  I convinced Nicole to give Keith's dogs to Sue Ann because her family can give them more attention. Karla took our older cat, Lady Midnight, and she is doing fine outside. When they have Keith's two dogs in the same house, it will help all the pets. I was concerned about our young cat, which I had fallen in love with, but I knew I would not be able to give her enough attention.  I asked God to help me find a better home for her.
Keith had so much stuff, including two kayaks and many tools. I knew I wouldn't be kayaking by myself, so I gave them to my

daughter and son-in-law. I couldn't believe how much stuff we had accumulated. My friends came with a big truck and trailer, and they hauled out the discards. Jody and Karla made many more trips to the dump and thrift shop for me.

## 23. Blessings and Healing  (8-28-2008)

The Holy Spirit has helped me focus on God's blessings and what I have received from Him in the midst of mourning and grieving. This brought much healing to my heart.

When I was leading chaplain's worship service, I asked people to share how they were thankful for God.  He has touched many people. A man in A4 broke down in tears, and many from A3 were touched by the Holy Spirit.

God blesses us when we finally learn to focus on God's goodness. We focus on our needs too much, and we tend to pray to receive something from God. He is teaching me that we need to be thankful for what we have already received, so we can recognize God's grace in our lives. When God is honored, the Holy Spirit blesses people, and that's what was happening.

## 24. Prayer and Distraction  (8-29-2008)

After I made an offer to buy the house, I started thinking about how I needed to fix it up. I can live in a beautiful environment. However, the thoughts of remodeling distracted me from my prayer. Instead of praying, my mind drifted into how I could remodel. I asked God to forgive me.

## 25. No Dinner Out  (8-30-2008)

I wrote a weekly devotion for the Upper Room.  I was glad that they asked me to write, because I can share stories from a jail chaplain's point of view. Many people do not have exposure to the stories of the inmates, so I picked out some powerful inmate leaders' stories of transformation.  I would be paid for this writing assignment. When I received the check, I was going to take Keith out to dinner and surprise him, because he was a tremendous help with my English. I wanted to make him happy and show him my appreciation, but he is gone. That made me really sad. I decided that I should ask God what I should do with the money.

The first time I received money for my writing, I was attending Portland Community College.  I wrote a short story about my sister's death for a Creative Writing class.  Our teacher gathered the students' stories and put them in a publication called <u>Pointed Circle</u>, and they sent me a check for my story. I took Keith out to dinner with the money, because he helped me a lot while I was attending school.

One thing Keith and I enjoyed was going to different restaurants. Before our kids came along, we used to celebrate our wedding anniversary every month on the 15[th.] Sometimes we pretended that we were dating. He would go out and come back later to pick me up and take me out to dinner. That was fun. Also, whenever I found a good restaurant, I took Keith there so he could enjoy the food, and he did the same.

The last time Nicole came with her three kids, I took her out shopping, then for lunch. While I was eating, I became sad and was in tears, realizing that I couldn't take Keith out anymore when I found a good restaurant. I did not realize how much I had to adjust my way of thinking and my lifestyle. I shared with my daughter how much it was hurting me to know that I couldn't take Keith out, and he couldn't take me out anymore.

## 26. Joyful Heart  (8-31-2008)

I had to cancel some church invitations to share about the TPPM. I was hurting badly, so I told them I would visit later. A church in Colorado Springs invited me when my spirit was high, so I went with my friend, Laura, and gave a presentation. I was encouraged about how supportive they were of this project. "Thank you, Lord, for helping me share this project to help inmates."

As I was going home after the presentation, the thought of going home to an empty house hurt me. I felt sad that Keith had to live in my memory only. I did not want to go home and feel the sadness and self-pity.

Most of the time when I arrived home from work, Keith was already there because his office was at home. I missed seeing his truck. The thought of not being able to see him was hard to accept. I felt lonely as I walked into the room, meeting only silence. I knew if I let my sadness set in my heart, it wouldn't do any good. I thought about how lonely Jesus feels when we only focus our thoughts on people. I began to understand why the Holy Spirit kept asking me to spend more time with the Lord. In order to be healed, I have to spend more time with the Lord. "Lord, thank you for taking care of me. I even thank you for the silence in my home."

After prayer, my heart was filled with overflowing peace, joy, contentment, and gratitude. This reminded me of what David had written in Psalm 23:1, *"The Lord is my shepherd and I shall not be in want."* God fills my empty heart with the Holy Spirit. He taught me how to cope with sadness and depressed feelings by thanking God for His grace. He has the power to heal broken spirits and fill lonely hearts with joy. I can praise Him for His goodness and compassion. There is no time to suffer from self-pity. If I had died before Keith, he would be walking this path of grief and pain. I thanked God that He was letting me walk this road of suffering even though it is a road of tears. I believe there is a reason for me to walk this road and He has a lesson to teach me.

## 27. Jesus' Tears (9-1-2008)

The Lord gave me a vision. My head was leaning on Jesus' lap and I was crying. Jesus' tears were falling on my head. I said, "Lord, Jesus, I love you. You have blessed me so much, but I ignored you for so long. Don't feel lonely, Jesus. I am here for you. You are always available as long as I am available to you. What a blessing it is to know you. Let me love you, Jesus. Let my love for you put a smile on your face. Let my love bring healing in your lonely heart."

Today, after worship service at ACDF, I did not want to go home. I had dinner with Fletcher. He asked me how I was doing. I talked about my grieving process, what made me cry, and what brings healing to me. I was thankful that I had a son who understood my need to spend time with someone with whom I could talk about Keith.

## 28. Testimony (9-2-2008)

I was working on a weekly devotion for Upper Room, "Reflections" and was encouraged. I was preparing stories of transformation through inmates' stories and my own. God can bring healing to our hearts as we share our stories of transformation. I wrote how God was helping my grieving process for the inmates. My story is also God's story of how He helped me.

## 29. Grieving Heart (9-3-2008)

Yolanda came to help me with packing, and I asked her to help me with editing my devotion as I cleaned the basement. After that, Yolanda loaded the *Maximum Saints* books in her car to send them to prisons. She also loaded five boxes in my car so I could mail them to prisons. I was encouraged by her. She used to be a volunteer at ACDF but now works at her church to help people in halfway houses. She is effective and compassionate.

After Yolanda left, I had no motivation to stay home. I spent lots of time in shopping centers and did not go home. That made me cry. No one and nothing can replace Keith. I was crying at the furniture store and at Target. I just couldn't stop the tears. I learned that grieving is hard. In every thing and every moment, anything can be a trigger for sadness. I can associate any situation with missing Keith. Obviously, I had to go through this process. There was no other way or escape from the path of pain and suffering. "Lord, please heal my grieving heart."

Tomorrow is Keith's birthday, but I can't say "Happy Birthday." This made me cry more. I bought yellow roses and put them in the living room to celebrate Keith's birthday. It made me feel better. I was able to do something for him.

## 30. Keith's Birthday (9-4-2008)

I did not tell anyone that today was my husband's birthday, because I did not want others to know. I did not have the heart to lead worship because of my tears. I called one of the volunteers to find out if he could lead worship for me. He did not answer the phone. So, I led the worship and God blessed the people who came. Worship is the highlight of my day because of the Holy Spirit's anointing in the worship services. Today, I had this big empty heart and asked God to fill it with His love and my love for Him. I know He is taking care of Keith, but this knowledge did not seem to help me. My pain was too great. It was good I got the flowers for Keith. It's a reminder of how I treasured him while he was alive and after he died. I knew that if he were alive, he would be happy.

## 31. A New Birthday (9-5-2008)

Yesterday was hard because it was Keith's birthday. The yellow roses were beautiful. "Lord, thank you for Keith's new birthday in heaven. July 9 was his first birthday in heaven. That was the day his body died, but his spirit went to heaven with the Lord. I believe he had a warm welcome and celebration. Now, every day is a celebration for him in heaven with the Lord Jesus. Thank you, God, for taking care of him."

## 32. A Symbol (9-6-2008)

I called my sister-in-law, Jeaneane, and told her how hard it was not to be with Keith on his birthday. I was crying as I was telling her about how I was grieving. Jeaneane and I had a nice talk and that helped me. In the midst of grieving, God has been speaking to me,

*Dancing in the Sky*

saying that someday I will be filled with so much joy. I asked, "How can I be filled with joy when my husband is gone?" God said, "You will know it when it happens. You will know that it came from me." God gave me hope and something to look forward to in the future.

My husband's churches have a new pastor, Rev. Dawnmarie. I don't have the heart to see her because she is a reminder of what I have lost. Helen invited me to a Sunday reception for the new pastor. She thought it would be a good idea for me to be there, but I declined. I told her that I am a symbol of grief to many people. Many in Keith's congregations are still grieving. If I were to go to the new pastor's reception, instead of it being a joyful occasion, I would be a reminder of their loss. I also told Helen that this new pastor is coming into a very difficult situation. I don't need to be a hindrance for her. Helen seemed to understand what I was saying and told me that I was very thoughtful.

## 33. Two Months Later  (9-9-2008)

It has been two months since Keith passed away. He has been transported to heaven. He graduated from this life. "Thank you, Lord, for the hope of eternal life. Thank you for your grace."

I overstretched my left arm about five months ago. About two weeks ago, I was having lunch with Fletcher, and he did not look happy. I asked him if anything was bothering him. He said yes, then said that I should go to a physical therapist for my arm so I don't have to wear my arm support. My doctor thought the arm support would help heal my arm, but it did not. I told him I planned to see a physical therapist after I moved to the new house. He insisted that I see a physical therapist sooner. Today I took his advice and saw a doctor for my arm. I did not realize I was in such bad shape. They showed me some exercises to help my arm.

When I met with Fletcher, he told me the University of Hawaii had accepted him for a medical school program. He wouldn't have to pay out-of-state tuition because he was a student at Metro State College. He said he would like to start at the new school by the next quarter. He was concerned about me and asked what I thought. I said, "Go for it. I think it's a great idea. You don't need to worry about me. I will be fine. You need to do what you want to do, and not let anyone or anything stop you. It's a good idea to go to different places. You can learn so much, and you can have a broader perspective. I changed after I came to America. The best thing that happened to me is that I have a broader perspective of life because of my encounter with culturally diverse people. You will love Hawaii. It's a beautiful place. I loved it when I visited there. It's a different culture there. You will learn a lot."

Not long after that conversation, I had a dream that Fletcher was with his friends saying he wanted to go to the University of Hawaii, but he was concerned about me and was changing his plans. Later, Fletcher told me that he decided not to go. Instead, he was applying to the University of Colorado because they have the programs he wants. He wants to go to medical school and C.U. seems to have a better program for that. Fletcher was accepted at C.U. and the campus is right next to Metro State in Denver, so he didn't have to move.

### 34. A Spiritual Doctor (9-10-2008)

I wasn't ready to go back to my book project because I still needed more healing. The remodeling, working at ACDF, and the hospital consumed most of my time and energy. I spent a lot of time shopping. For the first time I realized that there are many beautiful things with which to decorate my home. I felt badly because all my focus was on making my house beautiful. I also understood how people can easily spend money, time, and energy for beauty, but can forget about those who are suffering. Another lesson I learned is that if others can create beauty by using their gifts and doing their job well, then I should also have a higher goal of helping others as a minister.

I spent lots of time and energy buying decorations for the new house, and it helped me forget about the pain of losing Keith for awhile. "Lord, help me focus on you so I can love you and serve you as I should. Also, you are teaching me that I could be a better servant, as I see others who are good at what they do. Help me so I can be an effective minister and bring healing to many." All things, including family and friends, are temporary gifts. I wonder how Jesus would see me now. God spoke to my heart, "My daughter, you even have to watch out for good things because they can become distractions in your spiritual journey." The lesson I learned from this is that I have to make an intentional effort to focus my heart on God.

My son wants to be a doctor someday. I told him that I was a spiritual doctor. He smiled at that. I told him it is true. People come to me and tell me where it hurts. I prescribe God's Word and guide them to experience spiritual healing. God can bring healing, and that's what others need to hear. I told him that is the reason why I created the 100 Day Prayer Project for different spiritual healings.

### 35. Hope (9-11-2008)

Sally Shuler, former editor from the South Weld Sun, sent me a

*Dancing in the Sky*

copy of the newspaper with an article about Keith and a CD of digital pictures from the funeral reception. She was so thoughtful. I am thankful that there is hope that I can see Keith in heaven some day and I don't need to worry about where his spirit is.

## 36. Desire (9-12-2008)

This week I have been asking inmates to pray for the impossible in worship services. How can we have faith in God if we don't stretch our imagination? Our vision is too small, God has to stretch our minds to see what He can do through us. I asked, "What do you really want to see in your life? You know something that you want, but you think it is impossible. That's what you need to ask for." I realize how little love I have for Jesus since I keep resisting the thought of spending five hours a day with the Lord. I prayed, "Lord Jesus, I need you to help me to have more love for you so I can spend more time with you. Please help me to follow what you are asking me to do. You deserve my love and I recognize how little I love you."

## 37. Sense of Beauty (9-13-2008)

Something happened during this grieving process. My sense of beauty has deepened. I see beauty in people, things, and nature more than ever. God has helped me to experience the beauty of people through their good hearts and compassion, which they showed me after I lost my husband. God also has helped me to see beauty in things in which I did not pay much attention before, like nature, furniture, and even color and shape of pillows. Beauty brings healing to me. God created human beings who could feel pain, but also feel beauty to experience healing. Experiencing God's beauty through nature, His unconditional love, and kind people continue to bring healing to my grieving heart.

I noticed that I seem to forget things easily because I cannot focus. I have to work hard to remember. I wondered if that is one way our minds handle grief and loss. At some point, we have to forget about our pain. Until we can forget about it, sometimes it is difficult to let things go. I asked God to help heal my memory.

## 38. In the Right Place (9-14-2008)

I told Helen I was at the right place in my grieving process to receive support and encouragement. I was able to focus on healing my grieving heart because church friends took care of a lot of things like cleaning, packing, hauling garbage, and writing thank you notes for me.

Helen agreed. I cannot function well until I experience healing from this pain. God gave me hope by reminding me that I will be filled with joy. I asked Him if He was referring to my new home. He said, "No, it's much more than that. You will know it when it happens, and you will know it is coming from me."

### 39. Silence and Healing (9-16-2008)

Since God has kept asking me to spend five hours a day with him, I asked, "Lord, I am leading worship services five days a week and lead twelve worship services every week. Does that count?" I felt that my time was too tight, and I was telling God why I couldn't spend five hours with Him. The Lord said, "No. That doesn't count." He wants me to spend more time alone with Him than I have been.

Too many words in my mind become a distraction when I try to focus on the Lord. This morning, I enjoyed listening to God in silence. Silence brings healing. All the hurtful and negative thoughts have no room when there is silence in my mind.

When I was living in Glasgow, God asked me to listen in silence one hour every day. It's hard to wait in silence. As I practiced more, it got easier. I love my relationship with the Lord. He is always very encouraging.

### 40. Memories (9-17-2008)

This morning I drove to a field in Keenesburg, parked by the road and watched the sunrise. A man in a truck came and told me that I was on his property, so I drove to another spot to watch it. I have seen pictures of beautiful sunrises, but this was the most beautiful sunrise I've ever seen. God is awesome! He created it just with words. It's great to see what God can do.

I went back home, and started cleaning Keith's bathroom. There were many memories of Keith: his medicine box, his crosses, his contact lenses, his sophisticated scale, the wall he decorated with flowers, and the bathroom rugs, which Keith changed according to Christian seasons. He died during the Pentecostal season, and all the bathroom rugs were red. I tried to clean as fast as possible so I wouldn't break down and cry. I cried a lot last night and did not want to cry anymore. I tried to hold back my tears, but I couldn't.

I wanted to find out how I could resize Keith's wedding ring. The jewelry store told me they couldn't make it smaller because of the design. I told my daughter that she could have my ring when I die. She liked the idea. I haven't said anything to my children about Keith's ring. I don't want to give it to anyone. I decided to keep it for myself.

As moving time gets close, my mind gets busy with how I can remodel because the carpet needs to be replaced and the bathtub has a hole. This becomes distracting in my prayer time. I asked the Lord to forgive me. I knew I needed to finish the remodeling as soon as possible, so it wouldn't distract my prayer time. God spoke to me, "My daughter, don't worry about moving. I will bless you and give you an open door with your ministry. I will help you."

## 41. Decision (9-18-2008)

I said to Fletcher, "I feel bad for buying a big house when there are many homeless people out there suffering. Maybe I should look into buying a small home." Fletcher replied, "No, Mom, don't do that. You deserve nice things." I was thankful for my son's thoughtfulness.

Again, I tried to come up with some reasons why I should not buy this house. I started thinking about how much I had to remodel. I didn't understand why I didn't see these things at first. As I was thinking, God told me that if I help these people by purchasing their house, He will also help me when I decide to sell my house. I couldn't believe it. I did not realize He wanted me to buy this house until today. I couldn't change my mind. I knew if God did not want me to buy it, He would have told me.

## 42. A Book Assignment (9-19-2008)

I had a dream that I was teaching a man how to forgive. He seemed to be doing all right, and I was happy. God spoke to me when I woke up, "My daughter, you need to work on a book about forgiveness." I replied, "Thank you, Lord, for your direction."

One of the future _Maximum Saints_ books will have forgiveness stories. I started asking inmates to write a testimony of how God has helped them to forgive.

I taught a forgiveness class at Denver Women's Correctional Facility in 2000. I thought about writing a forgiveness book, but I wasn't ready. I was busy working on other books. I am grateful that God is helping me focus. There are many forgiveness books published on the outside. In order to bring them to our facility someone has to donate them. The only forgiveness book we can hand out is a book written by a non-Christian, which is not complete because it doesn't mention God's healing power. If I can write it with the help of the inmates, then we can send it to many other jails and prisons to help the incarcerated. God is the source of forgiveness. He has the power to help us forgive. Many inmates and I have experienced that God can help people release their resentments, anger, and bitterness. He can transform a violent person into a gentle and kind person when they can forgive. I've seen it many times.

God told me to write a book on dreams in 2000 and I added some of my dreams and interpretations to *Journey With Jesus*. In 2005, God told me that I should make a separate dream book, and I have been working on that. At this point, I still cannot work on any book project. Since Keith's death, I have been in so much pain that I haven't been able to concentrate. I know I have to wait for my heart to be healed.

### 43. Nature and Healing (9-20-2008)

I went to the elementary school to see the sunrise. It was a great sight. I have been busy for many years. I forgot to enjoy the beauty of nature. I wanted to visit Barr Lake because I enjoyed the time I spent there with Keith. When Fletcher came home, we went to Barr Lake. I really enjoyed being there. Keith and I walked around the lake and kayaked there many times. I have wonderful memories of that place. I just couldn't believe Keith would not be there anymore. I will be moving out by the end of the month. I thought I should make an attempt to meet the new pastor, Rev. Dawnmarie. I had not made an attempt to visit her or call her before, because it was too painful for me. When I was outside the house, I heard noises from the education building. The youth from Community UMC were playing outside as they had done many times when Keith was alive. I felt sad that Keith could not be there with them anymore. When I arrived at the education building, no one was outside. I did not want to go inside. If I did, I knew it would be hard for me and the youth group. Keith had a wonderful youth group that loved him. I did not want to remind them of their loss.

### 44. The New Pastor (9-21-2008)

I went to James Memorial UMC to attend worship service and meet the pastor, but I couldn't go in. I was overwhelmed with grief and turned around and left in tears. I then realized that I was not ready to meet her in the church where Keith ministered.

### 45. Beauty (9-22-2008)

I learned that I can be distracted by many things in my walk with the Lord. Even my hardship and grieving can consume much of my time and energy. When that happens, I don't have the time and

*Dancing in the Sky*

energy to focus on God. Even good things can be a distraction and hinder my relationship with the Lord. I need to watch out so I don't spend too much time seeking and experiencing the beauty of nature. I don't want to forget about Christ's beauty. Even though beauty brings healing, natural beauty or things created by humans are limited. The ultimate healing comes from God through the Holy Spirit's power. "Lord Jesus, I now realize why you are asking me to spend five hours with you to experience your beauty so I can experience healing."

### 46. Grieving and Pain (9-23-2008)

I went out to see the sunrise and listen to God. "My daughter, I made everything. Everything in it is mine. I will take care of you." I cried. I prayed, "God, heal my broken heart so I can love you and keep my attention on you. I don't know how long I have to grieve, but this is too painful. I can't grieve anymore. I need you to heal me."

### 47. Chaplain Sharon French (9-24-2008)

I visited Chaplain Sharon French at the Larimer County Detention Facility on the way home. She took me out for dinner and comforted me. I gave her some of the *Maximum Saints* books, and she was happy about that. She gave me a check for $50 for the Transformation Project Prison Ministry. She always has been kind to me and generous with the Transformation Project.

### 48. Letting Go (9-25-2008)

I called Rev. Dawnmarie and told her that I would like to meet her. She said she was close to my driveway, and within five minutes she was in my home. We had a nice talk. She was compassionate and encouraging. I was crying when I talked about how bad I felt because I was not able to help the church people.

I told her that Keith had always prepared his congregation to receive a new pastor and did extensive preparation when a woman pastor followed him, but this time he couldn't do anything about it.

She talked about how hard it was for her to follow a "favorite pastor." She said if Keith hadn't died, she wouldn't be ministering to these two congregations. That makes it hard for some of the grieving people to accept her as a pastor. She told me she wanted to come and visit me earlier, but she wasn't sure if I wanted to see her. I told her I wasn't ready to see her at that time, so it was good that she did not come to see me. Now, I wanted to see her and was glad that she came. I asked her if she would bless my new home, and she said she would be happy to do so.

I told her that she will be a great role model. As a woman, her ministry is needed in a congregation where the men have been leaders for so long. She will be an inspiration to many people, especially young girls who do not have the courage to follow God's call. I was glad that we were able to talk. We talked about how we will have more time to get to know each other better at the UMC Clergy Retreat.

After Dawnmarie left, I went to the physical therapist. The doctor told me I had frozen my arm and I needed to exercise it to loosen it. My arm is improving and I don't have to wear my arm support anymore.

Today was my closing day. I was very sad and was crying even before I went to the office to sign the papers, because Keith wouldn't be able to share the house with me. After I signed the papers, I went to work, but I did not have the desire to lead worship because I was hurting. I wanted to go to Barr Lake to get away. I called volunteers, but I couldn't find anyone. The anointing of the Holy Spirit was evident in worship and many were blessed. During prayer time, I asked the inmates to ask the Lord if there was anything He wanted to talk to them about.

I asked the Lord if there was anything He wanted to tell me. God reminded me of my aunt in Seoul, Korea. When I visited her three years ago, her husband had passed away. She shared that after his passing she asked God to take away any thoughts about her husband so she could go on with her life. She experienced a miracle. She was released from pain and suffering and did not grieve anymore.

God told me that I was holding on to my husband and was not willing to let him go. If I truly wanted to experience healing from pain and grief, I had to make a decision. I was not ready.

I had a dream that Keith was trying to make an excuse not to be with me anymore, but I felt his desire to be with me was there. It was healing for me to understand his love for me. Why did I have this dream? God said, "My daughter, I will bring healing in your heart. I will help you let him go, so you will be able to do what I want you to do."

My thoughts about Keith are taking up too much of my time and energy. It is hindering my ability to focus on our loving God. "Lord, help me to let go of Keith."

I was making plans to surround myself with Keith's stuff and to make a place to honor him when I moved into my new home. One wall would be dedicated to Keith with pictures of him and his life. Also, I would plant a memorial tree in the backyard. I was going to grieve for Keith until I died to remind myself that Keith's spirit is with me. I thought that would bring healing to me.

I was surprised when the Lord told me not to bring Keith to my new home. I taught many people how to grieve and asked them to let their loved ones go, through prayer. But, in reality, I was the one holding on. This journey of grieving was so new to me. It was different from losing my sister or my father. Keith and I had shared our dreams and planned our future for a long time, and all that had to go. I needed to follow God's suggestions. That is easier said than done.

I tried to remind myself that Keith is with the Lord. He is worshiping, dancing, and making others happy with his humor. Though I believe this, I still wasn't ready to give him to God. He is telling me that I need to prepare for my future life with Jesus, not with Keith. "God, I made a decision to let go of my desire to share my life, beautiful things, nice things, and even hard times with my husband. I let go of my wishes, self-pity, hopes, dreams, expectations, and everything that is related to him. Please take away my desires, wishes, and everything that is associated with Keith." I still felt I wasn't ready to let go of Keith. I wanted to go to my new house, but did not, because I was still holding on to him.

# Chapter Three: God Repaired My Broken Dam.

## 1. Grieving Plans  (9-27-2008)

God reminded me again that I should not bring Keith to my new house. God gave me a vision. I was tightly holding a clear plastic balloon shaped like Keith, and Jesus was standing by the door of my new house, waiting for me. Jesus was ready to lead me into the next stage of my life, but I wasn't ready to follow Him. God confronted me with my distraction from my spiritual journey with Him because of my grieving. Then I knew that I had to let go of all my plans to grieve for Keith. "Lord Jesus, I let go of my plans, expectations, desires, regrets, self-pity, hopes, and dreams related to Keith. Please heal me and take away all desires that are related to him, so I can be healed from my grieving heart."

After I prayed I felt I was ready, and I went into my new house with a new plan to spend more time with the Lord. Spending more time in prayer is an assignment God has given me. He is encouraging me to spend more time with Him, so I can find peace, joy and be healed from my grieving heart.

## 2. Moving  (9-28-2008)

I was happy that Rev. Dawnmarie's daughter would be able to take our cat, Joan. The cat did not come out when I left for my new home. She was hiding somewhere.

Jody told me I did not have to clean the parsonage. The church people would clean it. Anything I did not want, would be taken to a thrift store or to the dump. That was a blessing.

At first, I was going to rent a big U-Haul truck to move, but Donald Morgan and Deputy Ty Nazarenus volunteered to help me move with their horse trailers. So, I accepted their offer. Deputy Nazarenus' wife, David and Jody's family, and Karla's family came to help. All together, I had eleven friends, and Fletcher helped me. Angela and Dan were painting even before I moved into my new home. They were thoughtful. It took three hours to load everything and less than 30 minutes to unload it. I thanked God for them. Afterwards, we had pizza and had a great time visiting.

## 3. The Sunrise  (9-29-2008)

I decided to have a prayer room upstairs. I saw the beautiful sunrise from there. I was thankful that I did not have to drive anymore to find a place to watch the sunrise.

I went to the parsonage to pick up some more belongings, and when I called the cat, she came to me. I was glad to see her, but then she ran away from me. I called her but she did not come out. Dawnmarie's daughter was going to pick her up that morning. I was going to put Joan in a cage. I called Karla and she brought a wire cage. I almost had given up finding the cat and was ready to leave when she came out. I patted her. Putting her in the cage, I said good-bye to her and left. I was glad that she would be taken care of. I thanked God that He answered my prayers to find a good home for her.

## 4. Feeling Blessed (9-30-2008)

I saw the sunrise from my prayer room again. It was glorious. The sky was colorful and gorgeous, even though there were many houses outside the window. I also saw planes in the sky and that made me happy. I grew up by an American Air Base where I saw planes flying all the time. One of the things in life I wanted to do but decided not to is learn how to fly. Now, when I look at planes in the sky, I think about the visions people must have had to create the planes. Someone thought about making planes when many people thought it was impossible. I would like to dream the impossible like those people. With God, we can do so much more than what we can think or imagine. I asked God to enlarge my vision of my ministry so that many more prisoners could get help through the TPPM. I have many wonderful friends helping me. They all have the same heart to help the incarcerated who are in need of God's grace and salvation message.

The idea of enlarging my vision came from God. While I was attending Iliff, I used to pray, "Lord Jesus, I am yours. Use me to the maximum. Help me to bring many people to Christ." I prayed this same prayer many times. Then one day I went to church to pray and God asked, "How many people do you want to bring to Christ?" I couldn't believe what I heard. I had to think for a while. I thought I should give him an impossible number. I replied, "I would like to bring one million people to Christ." At the time, it looked impossible, but as time passed, I could see that there is a possibility. God started sending me to many prisons and jails to share Christ while I was attending Iliff, and there was a reason for that. God was teaching me I have to act on what I pray and what I want to see. If I just pray and not do anything, there is no way I could work toward my dream and vision of saving many souls.

*A Story of Hope for Grieving Hearts*                                    67

When I was working on the *Maximum Saints Never Hide in the Dark* book project in 2008, I started raising funds for this book. By the time the book was ready to send to the publisher, I was able to raise funds for 1,500 copies. That should have been enough for ACDF since we have 1,100 male and 200 female inmates. God challenged me by telling me that my vision was too small. Because of that, I ordered 10,000 copies and then actively went out and raised the funds. My plan was only having one Maximum Saints' book but God challenged me to have a bigger vision to publish more books and produce DVDs.

Last year, God told me again, my vision was too small. If my vision and dream of bringing one million people to Christ was too small, what was God thinking? I have been praying that God will help me understand His vision and plans for me so I can have His vision and work toward it. As my faith grows, I can see why God is challenging me to have a bigger vision. Without having vision to see something, I would not try to make it happen. I am still praying, "Lord, help me to dream the impossible and let me also have the faith to make it happen with your help."

## 5. My Mother  (10-2-2008)

My mother and brother came from Los Angeles and helped me a lot in my new home. Rev. Kristi, my brother, and Angela helped me with painting. My mother cooked food for my Korean friends, and we had a great time. She cooked more food and put it away in the freezer and told me to eat it later. I am so proud of my mother. Because of her prayers, I believe God has blessed me with many ministry opportunities. I told my Mom, "I won't have anything to receive when I get to heaven. I have already received so many blessings here." She replied, "No, you will be rewarded a lot. You will have a crown because you are helping many people." My mother is always so encouraging. I am blessed to know that she is proud of me. She always treats me with respect and love. When I was a teenager, one of my friends came to visit my home. She told me how she was impressed by my mother because my mother treated me with such respect. My mother has been that way with all her children.

I am grateful that my mother sent me to church when I was little. I found God because of her. She planted the seed of faith in my heart through her faithfulness to the Lord. My father treated her badly because he didn't want her to go to church. She kept her faith and attended church. Her love for the Lord and the way she lived and how much she loves her children inspires me. She could have been a pastor if she had the chance to have a higher education. She couldn't but God used her mightily in my life. I learned about God and faith from her more than any other pastor I had met. When I decided to go into the ministry, she encouraged me the most.

I used to say that my mother could have been perfect if she had divorced her abusive husband because our whole family suffered because of my father's abusive behavior. Now I know she tried her best with what she knew. She is the perfect mother for me.

## 6. Temporary Gifts (10-3-2008)

Since I moved into my new home, I have been busy painting, cleaning, and unpacking boxes. I even cleaned the leaves from the lawn. It was good exercise. I let go of all the plans to grieve the loss of Keith. I did not make a corner to remember Keith. I decided not to plant a tree to remember him in the back yard, either.

I knew that if Keith were alive, there was no way I could have bought this house since he wanted a bigger yard for his pets. God taught me that I am on a journey with Him and not with Keith. I need to focus on how I can spend more time with the Lord.

I feel like I am in a retreat center when I am at home. My house is decorated with many angels, and I am reminded that angels are watching me and taking care of me. I plan to invite my family and friends to come and pray if they need a place to pray. I decided to fix a guest room for that purpose.

I prayed, "Please help me deal with my loss of Keith." God replied, "My daughter, it wasn't a loss. He wasn't yours anyway. He is mine, my child, no one else can claim him as theirs. Nothing you have is yours; it is all mine. Know that you own nothing. Everything you have is a temporary gift. When you know what you truly own, you will be healed from any distractions. You are a temporary keeper and manager of your house and furniture and everything else in it. You don't own your children. They are mine, also."

"Thank you, Lord, for helping me realize that."

Since I have given everything to the Lord, I have found great peace of mind. I don't dwell on Keith as much as I did before. I found a new life with Jesus. I can enjoy life and focus on God.

## 7. A Gift of Healing (10-4-2008)

I was busy with remodeling and suddenly realized that I am not grieving anymore. I am functioning normally just like before I lost Keith. When I was grieving, my mind was full of sad thoughts about him and there was no room for anything else. Grieving was a painful process, and I am not having that pain. I have calmness and peace in my mind. This has happened since I prayed to God to take away any thoughts associated with Keith before I moved into my new home.

I can't believe that I am healed from grieving. Since God healed me, I have not broken down, not even once, over the loss of Keith. There have been times that I shed tears when I was explaining to others what I have gone through because of my husband's death, but not like before when my heart was immersed in deep sorrow and pain.

I don't have triggers related to the loss of Keith any more. Seeing other couples does not make me grieve. Looking at Keith's pictures and stuff does not bring tears. When I drive, I don't dwell on his accident, but I enjoy driving. When I go home, I don't have to grieve that Keith is not there because I am convinced that Jesus is there with angels to greet me. When I am at my beautiful home, I feel the presence of the Lord, and I am filled with comfort, joy, peace and gratitude.

I did not think this was possible since I lost him less than three months ago. God has heard my prayers to let Keith go and is helping me focus on Jesus. I just have good memories of Keith. I truly believe that he is in heaven with God. This is God's doing, because before, even though I believed Keith was with the Lord, I had a difficult time rejoicing in it.

Now, I am able to focus on what I want to do. For the first time since Keith died, I was able to start the dream book.

I wonder what would have happened if I had not had to move. Would I have experienced healing that soon? As I thought about it, I believe God would have brought me healing in any circumstance. Certainly, this is a miracle that I did not expect or even thought would be possible.

I don't even have the desire to have Keith with me. When I feel lonely I don't get sad, but I go to God and start praising Jesus. Then God fills me with overflowing joy. God took away all the painful thoughts related to Keith. "Thank you, Lord Jesus, for healing my grieving heart." This is a gift of life that the Lord has given me, one of many chances to experience God's wonders, so I can love and serve Him.

## 8. Silence  (10-6-2008)

All of my family left. I love the silence at home. Whenever I am alone, I feel God's presence more than ever. I have peace, and my heart is filled with gratitude. "Thank you, God, for all the blessings you have given me."

## 9. Beyond Imagination (10-7-2008)

In my new home, I am able to sing, pray, and my thoughts are always on God. I listen to praise songs, and my heart is filled with thankfulness and gratitude. I feel I don't deserve this happiness, but God is the One who is filling my heart with overwhelming joy. I bought a bird feeder and put it in the backyard. For the first time, I hear birds chirping. I love watching them through the window. "Thank you, God, for the gift of this house." God said, "My daughter, I will bless you more than you can imagine. I'll take care of you beyond measure." I replied, "Jesus, you have blessed me so much already. How can you bless me even more?" He replied, "You only have a little taste of heaven. The time will come when you know how much love and power I have for you." I said, "Thank you, Lord. You are great!"

## 10. Delighted (10-8-2008)

I am delighted with how I can remodel with the help of many good people. I have received so many blessings from God, including my children and grandchildren. "Thank you, God, for all the blessings."

## 11. Broken Dam (10-11-2008)

This week at chaplain's worship services, I started sharing how God directed my healing process and what we need to do to experience healing for a grieving heart. Many inmates were grieving from a recent loss, and some have been grieving for a long time.

I explained that our hearts are like a reservoir where the water is calm in a normal stage. However, when we lose someone we love, it's like the gates of the dam are open. These reservoir gates have many gates and each door has a name like desires, self-pity, regrets, blames, unforgiveness, dreams, wishes, resentments, anger, and many thoughts associated with the person who died. As long as people suffer from any of these, they cannot function. Until they can shut all the gates, they cannot have peace or joy, nor can they help others who are hurting. That's what happened to me. I was constantly grieving with many triggers of pain, and there was no room to think about others' pain or have the energy to help them. I needed help in shutting these gates because I didn't know how. God showed me how to shut them by letting my husband go. God took away every painful thought associated with my husband's passing. My gates of grief were repaired by God.

*A Story of Hope for Grieving Hearts*                                                   71

One inmate was in tears and said, "Chaplain, I understand what you are saying now. God is asking me to let go of my mother. Could you pray with me, so I can let her go?" I prayed with her.

## 12. The Clergy Retreat (10-14-2008)

Two months ago, I wasn't sure if I should go to the clergy retreat because I was in so much pain. As it turned out I was glad I decided to go because God brought healing to my heart. This is the first clergy retreat to which I have gone without Keith. It was a blessing that Derek and Joy Detoni-Hill, a clergy couple, gave me a ride since I did not want to drive in the mountains in the winter season. I signed up to share a room, but I regretted this because I wanted privacy. Pastor Dawnmarie told me that she was staying at her friend's two-bedroom condo. She asked me to stay with her, so I went with her instead. I had a great time getting to know her, and I was able to work on my writing project.

Many friends expressed their concern for me and gave me encouragement. I told them I was doing well because God had brought healing. Some mentioned that most people believe that people cannot recover that quickly. I agree with them. I know I couldn't have healed if God had not directed my healing process. My grieving would have lasted for the rest of my life if I had done it my way. I have experienced many miracles in my spiritual journey, and this is one that I will never forget. I have more faith in God now because of this experience.

Losing Keith is a big loss for me, but God has taught me many lessons through this painful process. I understand what it means to lose someone you love and what it means to be immobilized with pain from grief. I also understand what it means to be healed with God's help and to go on in life without triggers or mourning.

I had a great time at this retreat because God helped me to focus on what I have. I have many clergy friends who care about me. I can smile, and I feel blessed.

While I was praying in worship, I asked the Lord how I was walking with Jesus. Jesus gave me a vision of a little girl dancing in front of Him. I knew the little girl was me. Now, I can truly say that God has lifted me from mourning Keith and has blessed me with the oil of gladness. I was anointed by Jesus with His tears. Now, I am dancing before Jesus because He fills my heart with joy.

The Scripture talks about how God brings joy (Isaiah 61:3): *"and provides for those who grieve in Zion -- to bestow on them a crown of beauty instead of ashes, the oil of gladness instead of*

*Dancing in the Sky*

*mourning, and a garment of praise instead of a spirit of despair. They will be called oaks of righteousness, a planting of the Lord for the display of his splendor."*

God restored my gladness and filled my heart with joy by helping me understand His grace and blessings in my life. I still have two beautiful children and the rest of my family who love me. God is taking care of all my needs and guiding my path with peace, joy, and hope. I am truly blessed.

### 13. Holding You  (10-16-2008)

The second day of the retreat, my assigned roommate left early, so I stayed in my room. I loved the silence. I need a lot of time to be alone so I can focus on God with no distractions. Spending time with God brings healing in my mind and heart.

The worship services touched me the most in this retreat. I was moved by a song played at worship: "I Want to Hold You Till I Die."

"Lord Jesus, I have decided to hold you till I die. I'm so happy with you. You are the only one to whom I can give complete love and devotion. I give you my life, my love and all I have, even my children and my future. Everything I have is yours. Thank you, Lord."

I see why He was asking me to spend more time with Him. "Thank you, God, for your wisdom. You knew what I needed. I need to pray more so I can win the spiritual battle against temptation and resist any distraction which hurts my relationship with you. I need you to help me in my spiritual journey. It's by your grace that I recognize this."

Even though I have faith in God and love the Lord, the devil tries to hurt me sometimes, especially when I'm asleep. This happened after my sister died in a car accident. I was terrified to go to sleep, but God delivered me from my nightmares. The devil sometimes tries to attack me in my dreams, but I am not afraid anymore. Now, I know how to fight. I believe the devil tries to attack me to disturb my peace.

While I was sleeping at this retreat, I felt the devil's attack for the first time since Keith died. I struggled because the devil's arm was very strong and would not let me go. I rebuked the devil in Jesus' name to leave from me, then I woke up. I asked the Lord Jesus to sit next to me and to protect me with warrior angels. I am glad that God helped me to sleep peacefully after that.

The devil tried to put fear in my mind, but I know his tactics and I have no fear because Jesus is stronger than he is. I remembered 1 Peter 5:7-11: *"Cast all your anxiety on him because he cares for you. Be self-controlled and alert. Your enemy the devil prowls around like a roaring lion looking for someone to devour. Resist him, standing firm in the faith, because you know that your brothers throughout the world are undergoing the same kind of sufferings. And the God of all grace, who called you to his eternal glory in Christ, after you have suffered a little while, will himself restore you and make you strong, firm and steadfast. To him be the power for ever and ever. Amen."* The devil wants to create turmoil in me, but it is not working because I have Jesus.

## 14. Which Song (10-17-2008)

The Holy Spirit filled me with joy as I was praising God. Whenever I can, I sing for Jesus. Jesus is pleased with it. A while back, I asked the Holy Spirit, "How can I love Jesus?" He replied, "Worship Him." So, when I go to pray, I ask the Lord, "Which song shall I sing for you, Lord?" The Holy Spirit will give me songs, and I sing for Jesus. I feel the presence of the Lord when I sing for Him. My heart is filled with gratitude and tears come.

## 15. Worthwhile (10-19-2008)

I remembered what Keith said to me a while back. He asked, "Was it worth it?" He was talking about my response to the call to ministry. Without hesitation, I replied, "Yes, it was worth it." I knew my family went through a lot because Keith did not want me to go into the ministry. I commuted 430 miles one-way every week to attend seminary for three years. My first year at Iliff, I almost died in a car accident on an icy road after a big truck passed me and covered everything with snow. I couldn't see anything. I lost the sense of direction and drove down the steep hill and it was a miracle that I survived. After that, I suffered from panic attacks whenever I drove on the icy road.

I made the choice and was determined to do what God asked me to do. God asked me for a 100 percent commitment to serve Him, and I told him I would do it. God gave me the urgency to respond to the call and no one understood it including my husband. I was spiritually dying at home and it affected my body. I couldn't believe what was happening. One day I had an experience when I was literally physically dying at home and through prayer, God brought me out of it.

I know our children paid a heavy price because I was gone a lot during their critical times. My decision at the time was based on my thought that in order for me to take care of our children later, I had to

74                                               *Dancing in the Sky*

obey the Lord. If I died spiritually, I thought I couldn't take care of them. Only people who have experienced spiritually dying can understand what I had gone through. My spirit came alive when I started ministry, and I finally realized that I was born to be a minister.

God blessed my obedience beyond imagination through my prison ministry. I finally learned what it means to find joy in loving and serving Him. God's outpouring of the Holy Spirit is blessing people who are hurting and broken in jails and prisons. God blesses me as I help those who are hurting and are in need of His healing presence.

When God first called me to the ministry, I struggled for more than a year. I told Him I didn't want to go into ministry, but I will write a book to help others to grow in faith. I wrote _Moment by Moment I Choose to Love You_, but God didn't let me rest. He told me that day with clear voice, "Go and tell others Jesus died for their sins and they are forgiven." I still wasn't ready. God was persistent and asked me to pray and read one gospel a day out loud for a year. Then I wrote another book, _Journey With Jesus_ and while I was writing, Jesus changed my stubborn heart. I finally realized the power of the Holy Spirit. That was a turning point in my life and I decided to go into the ministry. _Journey With Jesus_ was published while I was attending Iliff.

Then God helped me write _Journey of Mystical Spiritual Experiences_ while I was going through so many struggles because others didn't understand my calling. I was so filled with despair but while writing this book, God planted the seed of hope in my heart. I published it while attending school. I started distributing those books to jails and prisons to minister. That's how my book ministry started.

After I started working at ACDF in 2003, I struggled when inmates were asking for books. Chaplain's office didn't have enough books to distribute. So, I started Transformation Project, then I gathered inmates' stories and published three books: _Maximum Saints Never Hide in the Dark_, _Maximum Saints Make No Little Plans_, and _Maximum Saints Ordained by God_.

I preached at St. Elizabeth Episcopal Church, and the Holy Spirit's anointing and presence blessed me and those who came to worship. The church people donated $840 for the Transformation Project. Laura was there to help me.

Today, the Holy Spirit asked me the same question, "Was it worth it?" I replied in tears, "Yes, Lord, it was worth it. Lord Jesus, you are worth it. I would go into the ministry again if I were to live again. Thank you, Lord, for calling me to the ministry." Many times I asked Fletcher to forgive me for making him move to Keenesburg, because he did not want to move at first. It was difficult for him at the time, but in recent years, he said, "Moving closer to Denver was one of the best things that has happened to me. I could have gotten into trouble if we stayed in Buffalo."

## 16. An Open House  (10-20-2008)

I am happy and content with where I am. God is meeting all my needs, and I can say what Paul said. He wrote, *"And we know that in all things God works for the good of those who love him, who have been called according to his purpose." (Romans 8:28)* Keith's death was a tragedy for me and many others. I miss him, but I gave him to God. I am free from pain and a grieving heart. God helped me to recover. God saved me from anguish and all the destructive emotional turmoil. Now, I understand how people can die from a broken heart. In my case, I could have died in a car accident because my grief hindered my judgment.

When I was leading worship in F Module, the Lord said, "Ask whatever you want, and I will give it to you." This is the second time I have heard from the Lord that he will give me what I ask. The first time God asked me this question was in my first quarter at The Iliff School of Theology. I loved theological studies. I was going to enjoy seminary. After I finished school, I was planning to minister to prisoners. God spoke to me that I had my own plans, but I needed to know His plans, dreams, and visions for me. When I started asking for God's visions for me, He gave me faith that He will grant whatever I would ask. So, I asked God to help me understand Jesus' love. Then I had a spiritual experience I will never forget.

One day while I was driving, I felt that I was separated from the world and the world was full of people who were suffering and in pain. Their pain was so great that I felt their pain in my heart; I've never felt so much pain before, and I broke down in tears. God gave me an understanding that Jesus understood people's pain. He came to the world and died on the cross to save people from suffering and pain.

I understood Jesus' love because of that experience. Then a few days later, I saw a homeless woman on the street. I felt her pain, and I broke down again. I knew God was trying to tell me something. Two weeks later, I went to chapel and asked the Lord to guide my ministry. As I was leaving the chapel, Chaplain Lola West from Youth Offenders System (Y.O.S.) came and asked me to share my testimony at her facility. She told me that many inmates were touched by my book, *Journey With Jesus*. Before I went to Y.O.S., God spoke to me that He was looking for someone in whom He could entrust His power to transform people. I went and shared my testimony. For the first time in my life, I saw with my own eyes how the Holy Spirit can transform people's hearts. After that, I started organizing prison ministry at Iliff and took many students to eight different facilities. God has blessed me greatly through prison ministry.

This time, I knew what I wanted. I asked the Lord to give me more love for Jesus to make him smile.

I had an open house today. I invited my friends and asked them to bring a joke. I ordered pizza, since cooking overwhelms me because it is not my gift. Before I started working on removing carpet and extensive remodeling, I wanted to show my appreciation to those who helped me. Many friends came. They shared their jokes. We had a great time with a lot of laughter.

Rev. Dawnmarie led a prayer for the blessing of the house, and I felt the presence of the Lord. She was a blessing from God for my husband's congregations.

Later that evening, Fletcher came with his friend. They were so kind and nice to me. Fletcher hugged me twice and made me feel so special. "Thank you, Lord Jesus, for my wonderful son and for his love." The Lord blessed me so much today with the visit of many wonderful friends. I thanked God in tears.

## 17. My Family (10-22-2008)

I am so happy that God pulled me out of the river of tears. I know only He can do that. I was looking at pictures of Fletcher and of Nicole's family. They made me happy. "Thank you, Lord Jesus, for my family." I made reprints of a picture of Keith holding Nicole and Fletcher. Fletcher was only one day old. I made reprints for him so Fletcher can understand how much Keith loved him. When Fletcher saw the picture, he wanted to have it. I gave the picture to Fletcher and he looked happy.

## 18. Remodeling (10-23-2008)

I had a dream that two little dogs were with me, and one dog made a mess on my floor. I saw a beautiful dog that I was patting. I asked what this dream meant. God said to me that I need to try to get rid of distractions. At this point, my distraction is remodeling. I am so focused on it that I am distracted when I try to pray. "Lord, give me the wisdom to make the right decision so I can get it over with as soon as possible." God has been helping by sending people to help me remodel.

Decorating is not my gift. I am glad Angela is good with decorating. She has been helping me make the right decisions.

## 19. Distribution  (10-27-2008)

I went to a Colorado State Chaplains and Program Coordinators meeting and gave a presentation on the Transformation Project to make others aware of the books and DVD resources that we are producing. It was good that they finally approved TPPM books, but we cannot send the books to the state prisons until the chaplains contact the state coordinator. Colorado prisons have the highest prison population growth in the nation. TPPM used to send books to all of the Colorado state prisons, but this restriction will hinder that process.

I was disappointed about this policy because it will slow down distribution, but God encouraged me. He said, "My daughter, don't worry about distribution. I'm the one who is in charge of distribution, not the state." I need to rely on God for everything. In that meeting, I was warmly greeted by many program coordinators and chaplains who appreciated the books. I was very encouraged.

## 20. Numbered Days  (10-30-2008)

This morning, the Holy Spirit gave me a Scripture: "Your days are numbered." This is true for everyone. We will all die someday, and we need to be prepared. Only God knows how long we will live. This Scripture helped me to focus on God. We need to be accountable for what we have received and how we use it, especially our time. That's why God was telling me to spend more time with Him. In chaplain's worship, I asked inmates to share what they would do if they had only one more day to live. A wonderful discussion came out of that. Many don't even think about the short time we have on earth. We live as though we will live forever. I believe that is one reason why we grieve so much when we lose someone we love. Paul reminds us that we are all foreigners in this world. *"But our citizenship is in heaven. And we eagerly await a Savior from there, the Lord Jesus Christ, who, by the power that enables him to bring everything under his control, will transform our lowly bodies so that they will be like his glorious body." (Philippians 3:20-21)*

## 21. My Granddaughters  (10-31-2008)

I visited Nicole, but this visit was different from the last one. Last time I visited her, I was hurting so badly from grief and was so absorbed that I couldn't think about my daughter's family's healing.

This time, because God brought me healing, I was able to focus on how I can bring joy to my daughter's family, especially my granddaughters. First, I took Teila out for breakfast, then to a store so she could pick out gifts for her family. I had a great time with her. After that, I took Jamie out for lunch, then to a store, and she picked out gifts for her family. In this way, they can learn the joy of giving, and I was able to give them individual attention. They are so beautiful and precious.

In the afternoon, I drove to Tie Hack, a reservoir where Keith and I had kayaked. I walked around the lake, sat on a rock, and watched the beautiful mountains and the fish jumping in the lake. I sat there and thanked God for all the good things he has given me in my life, especially the good memories of Keith and our time there. It was such a healing moment. I could enjoy nature and be thankful, without breaking down, that Keith spent time with me on a beautiful lake when he was alive.

I was so focused on ministry that I usually did not think about how I could enjoy life. Keith had provided recreation through his many different hobbies. I loved kayaking because of Keith. My visit there was like saying good-bye to the lake. After that, I drove to Lake De Smet and enjoyed the beauty there. Keith and I also had kayaked there. We landed on a small island and enjoyed our time there. I thanked God that I was able to visit those places with a thankful heart instead of a grieving heart.

## 22. Grieving and Distraction (11-12-2008)

Today is my birthday. Last year I was working at ACDF on my birthday. Fletcher had surprised me by bringing special restaurant food to the facility after he and Keith went out for lunch. Fletcher gave me a hug which made me so happy.

Today, Fletcher and I went out for dinner, and I told Fletcher that God brought healing to my heart so much that I wasn't having triggers and was functioning normally. I also told him that it doesn't bother me to be alone because I enjoy the silence and spending time with God alone. He said, "That's good."

I had a dream that I had a nice new sleeper, but someone stole it. I was wearing old, dirty shoes. I told the restaurant that I lost my shoes and I was supposed to go somewhere, but I couldn't. I had this dream when I was so distracted with remodeling. I asked the Lord why I had this dream. He replied, "My daughter, many of my children have distractions like you do. You will learn to overcome them and you can teach others as well. Grieving is also distracting for many of my children. By teaching others that I can heal them, you will be able to help many to overcome distractions. I will give you wisdom to do all the remodeling so you will be able to spend time with me."

## 23. Many Prayers (11-18-2008)

Keith did not have any way of expressing his last wishes to the hospital staff. I decided to fill out Five Wishes for me, a form that explains what I want when I cannot express myself. I don't want anyone to revive me when my heart stops. I have seen so many people suffer in the hospital. As I started filling out the form, I thought that even though Fletcher is younger than Nicole, he should be able to carry out my decisions for me. He knows what I want and lives closer to me. Suddenly, I was flooded with tears and sadness overtook my heart. I was feeling my family's pain. I asked myself, "What would I do if I died and my family was overwhelmed with pain and grief?" I would pray for my family asking God to lift their grieving spirit and give them peace. I don't want my family to grieve to the point where they can't function like what happened to me. When I was overwhelmed with pain from grief, I couldn't think about anyone else. After God healed my grieving heart, I was able to think about how to help my children.

## 24. On My Wings (11-19-2008)

I had a dream that Keith was driving someone else's red pickup on an icy road. The top camper was broken, and he said he was in an accident. There was a baby inside that someone was holding. Somehow, I was on top of a high building watching this and wondering what to do. I could see Keith from there. I asked Keith if he got hurt, and he said he was okay.

This dream reminded me of the Scripture: *"Jesus said to her, 'I am the resurrection and the life. He who believes in me will live, even though he dies; and whoever lives and believes in me will never die. Do you believe this?"* (John 11:25-26) God is so real. Even though Keith's body died, his spirit did not die. "Thank you, Lord."

God spoke to me, "I will be taking care of you. You are on my wings." The Holy Spirit reminded me of two visions God had given me. First, Jesus helping me to dance. I am a little girl in this vision. Jesus' hand is holding my hand to spin. Second, Jesus gave me a round shaped, creamy white, beautiful flower for my head, like a crown. It made me happy.

I have set a high goal for TPPM, and I have been praying about this. God gave me confirmation for the first time. He told me that

*Dancing in the Sky*

someday I will be able to do it. I figured that if I don't have a goal, I will never reach it. I know it can be done if God allows it to happen, so I am glad that God is going to help me do it. My goal is to distribute at least 1,000,000 copies of *Journey With Jesus* to different jails, prisons, and homeless shelters. I told Fletcher about my goal. He asked, "How many have you distributed so far?" I replied, "About 12,000 copies but when the Spanish book comes out, it will be 22,000 copies." He said, "That's good."

## 25. The Criminal Justice Summit (11-22-2008)

I attended the Criminal Justice Summit in Washington D.C. It was organized by the General Board of Higher Education and Ministry of the United Methodist Church. Many gave presentations about aftercare. I gave a presentation about the Transformation Project. When I mentioned that TPPM is working on translating two books into Spanish to help the Hispanic inmates, some chaplains clapped with joy. They understand that there is a great need to have Spanish inspirational books.

This was the best retreat I have ever attended. I had a table set up for TPPM books and DVDs. Many chaplains requested books and DVDs. I met many United Methodist chaplains and volunteers who have the same heart to help the incarcerated and are concerned about aftercare for prisoners.

## 26. Understanding Another's Pain (11-23-2008)

God again gave me a vision of a girl with creamy white flowers on her head, and flowers in her hands. I knew God was showing me that I was that little girl. He blessed me so much with the beauty of the people in the workshop. They understand what I understand: the pain and suffering of the incarcerated and those who are released with no resources to help them succeed.

It's beautiful to understand another's pain and to try to do something about it. A while back, I prayed to the Lord that I wanted to see more healing in my ministry. God spoke to me, "Unless you understand other people's pain, you cannot bring healing." I am beginning to understand what God was talking about. If we understand other's pain, we cannot hurt others. But many times we just don't know how much we are hurting each other.

God spoke to me, "I will be a blessing to you, and you will go to many places. You will be filled with so much joy." "Are you talking about joy from remodeling?" "No, the joy I give you is much greater than that." *"The ransomed of the Lord will return. They will enter Zion with singing; everlasting joy will crown their heads. Gladness and joy will overtake them, and sorrow and sighing will flee away. 'I, even I, am he who comforts you.'" (Isaiah 51:11-12a)*

## 27. His Teaching (11-25-2008)

I have the desire to love my Lord Jesus. I learned that it's hard to know how to love Him. Telling Him how much I love Him doesn't seem to be enough. I see something is missing, and I don't know what it is. "Lord Jesus, teach me how to love you. Father God, teach me how to love you. Holy Spirit, teach me how to love you." I believe God will answer my prayers in His time. In heaven, we will have love for the Lord with no distractions and praise Him every moment, but I want to have it now.

I preached the book of Revelation a while back. In it Jesus told John to write letters to seven different church leaders. (Revelation 1:1-3:22) In the letter to Ephesus, Jesus said, *"Yet I hold this against you: You have forsaken your first love. Remember the height from which you have fallen! Repent and do the things you did at first. If you do not repent, I will come to you and remove your lampstand from its place." (Ephesus 2:4-5)* I wrote my love letter to Jesus to remind myself not to lose my first love because it happened to me once before after I neglected reading the Bible. I also asked the inmates to write their own love letters to Jesus. This is my letter:

Lord Jesus, I love you,

It's you Lord, Lord Jesus, I've been looking for you for so long, and I found you. Rather, I am found by you because of your grace and your great love for me. I love you Lord – I don't even have enough words to describe how much I love you. I can't even find a song that can describe my love for you.

As I look back to when I was not happy, it was my love for you that was missing. All these years I did not even realize that I was created to love you. My big empty heart was created for you to fill with your love. I was looking elsewhere to fill this empty heart, but thank you for bringing me to the place where I recognize your love, your grace and my need to love you.

For a long time, I was wondering how I could love you more, but I just did not know how. Now, I understand what love

*Dancing in the Sky*

is through the ministry you gave me. Love brings life, hope, passion, enthusiasm, excitement, fulfillment, joy, and peace. I love my ministry. It gives me so much joy, fulfillment, and excitement more than anything else. The Holy Spirit blessed me beyond imagination through my prison ministry.

The Holy Spirit reveals to me that my love for you has to bring life, passion, enthusiasm, joy, and excitement to you as well. Also, my love for you has to be the first priority in my life. I have this fulfilling life because you have given me many chances to make myself right with you. I learned that you want my love more than anything.

I made a decision to love you, my Creator, more than people, things, or even the ministry you created for your own glory. I declare to the world that no one, nothing, is more important than you. Lord Jesus, I love you. I honor you. I cherish you. I praise you. You are my everything. I pray that my love for you will grow every day. You fill my heart with joy. I pray that you will be pleased with my love for you, like a rose in your garden. I pray that I will be able to give you everything, completely, all that you have given me.

I made a decision to love you more than my sweet, fulfilling, joyful life-giving ministry. I understand that when everything, and everyone else is gone, you will be there with me always. You are the only one that matters because you will be with me till the end when no one else can. When I lose everything, even my breath, you will be with me, walk with me, holding me in your arms, carrying me to my permanent home which you prepared for me.

Let me love you, Jesus. Let my dedication to you and my service be pleasing to you. Let me be a blessing to everyone who comes in contact with me, like Abraham. Let me be a passionate and effective servant like Peter and Paul. Let me be a servant that you can use to the maximum for your glory. Let my service to you bring healing to many–many–too many to count. Let me see your smile today. Lord Jesus, I love you more than anyone and more than anything else.

Your beloved daughter,

Yong Hui

## 28. My People  (11-26-2008)

I had a dream that a big truck was running over people, but it did not crush them. I was very upset but couldn't do anything about it. God said, "My daughter, my people are strong, and they can move mountains."

Even though life is tough and many times we feel crushed by the disasters in life, God can help us be strong. This dream showed me that nothing can hurt God's people as long as they have hope in Him. There are things in life over which we have no control like losing loved ones. But grief and loss cannot hurt us when we experience healing from God. In fact, we can tell the world that God has the power to heal, and that is what I will be sharing with many people. Job lost everything he owned plus all of his children. He immediately worshiped God and praised God. I shared this in worship services. We need to learn from him how to handle disasters. That's the reason why I tell inmates who are going to sentencing to pray for miracles but always prepare for the worst. When we prepare for the worst, there will be no room to be upset or angry at God when we don't get what we have requested. Instead, we can thank Him in advance for His grace, because with God, we can handle difficult times, and we can come out strong.

## 29. Thanksgiving Day  (11-27-2008)

When Keith was alive, he cooked our holiday meals. He was an excellent cook and my family enjoyed it. I asked Fletcher if he was invited to a friend's home for Thanksgiving dinner, and he said, "No. All of my roommates will be with their families." I wanted Fletcher to have a family Thanksgiving dinner. I ordered a turkey meal from King Soopers that included everything. All I had to do was open the boxes and heat it in the oven.

Fletcher and his girlfriend along with two of my friends came and had dinner with me. I wasn't sure if I should pray before dinner because I wasn't sure about my son's girlfriend's faith. I had an uneasy feeling about it and I should have asked the Holy Spirit. Without asking I made a decision not to pray. The food turned out really good. Fletcher commented on how much he liked the food.

I was told that the first holiday is very difficult after losing your loved one. If God hadn't brought healing to my grieving heart, I know that Thanksgiving dinner would have been a disaster. I did not have to grieve. I enjoyed the dinner. There was a lot of laughter, and I had a great time with my guests. I thanked God for all the blessings.

At times I feel lonely because Keith is not with me, and those are the times I start praying and praising God. I thank God for what He has given me. Then, God fills me with peace and joy beyond imagination. I am truly blessed. I am glad that God taught me how to find peace and joy in worshiping Christ.

## 30. The Holy Spirit (11-28-2008)

This morning, God was after me because I did not lead the prayer before dinner last night. I should have known that it was the Holy Spirit convicting me, but I did not pay attention. Instead, I listened to excuses why I did not want to pray. I did not want to make my son's girlfriend uncomfortable. God said to me that I should not worry about what other people think about me, rather think about what God wants from me. He told me that I wasn't setting a good example as a minister of God.

I asked God for forgiveness in tears. I am learning that God is not going to let me get away with anything. I am glad that He is correcting me. Tonight, when my son and his girlfriend came to visit, I told them that God was after me because I did not pray. Fletcher told me he wondered why I didn't pray. I'm learning that I need to ask the Holy Spirit when in doubt. "Thank you, God, for the lesson."

## 31. A Mentor (12-3-2008)

I had a terrible dream about Keith and all I saw was his head on the road. When I woke up, I asked God why I had this horrible dream. God spoke to me that my children's losing their dad was so traumatic that it was more like what I saw in my dream. This made me cry for many days. I wept for my children. I asked God to bring healing to my children's grieving hearts.

When I was grieving, I wasn't able to understand how much my children suffered from the loss of their dad. I didn't realize how much support they needed from me. It's God's grace that He brought healing in me so I can understand how much my children need my attention and love. "Thank you, Lord, for opening my heart to understand my children's pain and suffering." God spoke to me, "Help your daughter, because at this point, her understanding of my love comes through you." I am thankful that God is helping me to see how much I need to help my daughter.

From time to time, God helped me to understand my children's pain when they were going through difficult times through my dreams.

Once I had a dream about my daughter when I was attending Iliff. My daughter was dating a man at the time, but I dreamt that my daughter was dating another man. After I woke up, I thought God was telling me what was going to happen to her.

That morning, I went to church to pray. God told me that my daughter needed a mentor to help her because difficult times were coming. I never thought about finding a mentor for my daughter until that day. God told me to ask Michelle Hannan to be my daughter's mentor. Michelle was attending First UMC where my husband was a pastor at the time.

I drove to Denver to attend school, and that night I called Michelle and asked her if she would be a mentor to my daughter. She told me that when our church was talking about how to be a mentor to youth, she immediately thought about my daughter. She said she would be glad to do it.

After that conversation, all through my daughter's high school years and many more years, Michelle took my daughter to her home every Wednesday night, fixed a meal for her, and spent time with her. I am forever thankful for what Michelle has done for her and my family.

Not long after Michelle started being a mentor for her, my daughter and her boyfriend broke up and she went through a very difficult time. I wasn't able to help my daughter because I was gone a lot, but Michelle did. I thanked God for helping my daughter. She had a tough time during her teenage years, and God helped her through Michelle. I will always be grateful for her generous and nurturing spirit.

## 32. God of Power  (12-7-2008)

I was leading D Module worship. Cindy, Paul, and Angela came. I had a vision during prayer. Jesus was holding my hands and standing on a high place. He gave me the understanding that his power can work throughout the world. I had tears of gratitude. In this worship, many were touched by the Holy Spirit.

God spoke to me, "My daughter, this is a little glimpse of what you will see in heaven." I said, "Lord, what can be better than being with you? Thank you for your love."

## 33. Surrender  (12-9-2008)

I try to pray the same prayer every day until God answers my prayer or He changes my prayer. My latest prayer is asking God to teach me to love Jesus. "Lord, teach me how to love you. I pray that there will be no distractions. My desire to love you will be granted. I surrender all my plans, passions, desires, dependencies, thoughts, expectations, and anything that is hindering my love for you. I love you,

*Dancing in the Sky*

Lord. Fill my heart with more love for you. Surround me with godly people who will help me to love you more. Surround me with warrior angels to protect me from anything or anyone who tries to get between you and me. Release me from all my distractions, whether they are people or things, so I can love you with a pure heart. Fill my heart with your love and my love for you. I love you, Lord Jesus."

## 34. Mija  (12-10-2008)

Mija called me and shared her joy. A while back she had heard God telling her to send $90 she had saved for an emergency to a man who was involved in a serious car accident. Mija's friend told her about him. Mija had been in a car accident herself. It almost killed her. She still can't work and is slowly recovering. She thought about sending him flowers instead of money, because she thought $90 was a small amount. God told her she should send the money, not flowers. She sent her friend a money order to deliver to the man. Mija's friend told her that she could not locate the address of this man. When the check was returned, Mija gave it to the local mission fund.

She was so thrilled that God communicated with her. However, she asked me why God would ask her to send money to a man when He already knew that he wouldn't be able to get it. I told her what was important was not the outcome, but her obedience. She agreed with me.

Mija asked me how I was doing. I told her that God brought so much healing in my heart that I'm not grieving anymore. She told me she had grieved for many years because her mother died when she was little. After she became a Christian, one day, she realized that she wasn't grieving anymore and did not miss her mother. Then she knew that God had healed her broken heart.

I was thankful she shared about the healing power of God. God healed me, so I understood what she was saying. "God, please heal our children from grieving hearts. I ask you to father them and help them to understand your love. Help all Keith's family and friends, so they can experience healing."

## 35. Temptation  (12-16-2008)

I learned something new. When I am distracted or tempted, I use it as a trigger to pray for others' salvation. This seems to work. Many times any distraction and destructive thoughts are caused by the devil, who is trying to discourage me in my spiritual journey with the Lord. I know I am in a spiritual battle. To win this battle, I need to learn how to fight and prayer seems to work.

I started teaching this concept in worship services and in my counseling sessions. Many inmates struggle with disturbing thoughts and feel helpless. The devil works hard to make people fall into sin by giving them negative thoughts. Since many inmates ask me how they can win over temptation, I tell them to use these thoughts as a trigger, as a reminder to pray for others' salvation. I said, "Confuse the devil by spending your time wisely. Instead of accepting the devil's suggestions and falling into sin, use them as a reminder to pray."

While I was praying at home, I had a vision of a house with two long lines going up to heaven. They were prayer lines. God spoke to me, "My daughter, it's good that you teach others to pray for salvation when they are tempted. Instead of following sinful desires, people can overcome temptation by praying to help others."

Prayer also brings healing when we are grieving because God hears our prayers. He has answered my prayers, and I am grateful for it.

# Chapter Four: My Cup Overflows.

## 1. My Calling  (12-23-2008)

I started asking inmates to find out what their calling was, before the new year. Then I asked the Lord what my calling was. The Holy Spirit gave me a clear understanding. My calling is to be a listener and cheerleader for the Lord Jesus. Why didn't I know this before? Now that I am in love with Jesus, I am more willing to follow the Holy Spirit. "Lord, help me to be a good listener and let me be a cheerleader for you." He said, "My daughter, you finally understand your call. You will be filled with joy when you learn to listen. You are in my hands."

When God called me to the ministry, I wasn't ready. At that time, the Holy Spirit guided me to pray. I learned that God did not just let me talk but that He wanted to talk. The Holy Spirit asked me to wait in silence and to listen.

The first time this happened to me, God helped me to see my attitudes that I had to change. The second time, God pointed out my pride attitudes, and I had to repent. Then God asked me to wait and listen one hour every day. That has been really challenging for me. During the time of listening, God was giving me spiritual visions. I asked Him for interpretation, and learned to listen more.

After we moved to Keenesburg, one day I heard God speaking to me, "Who would listen to Jesus?" I replied, "I will listen to Jesus." Then God spoke to me again, "Who would speak for Jesus?" I said, "I will speak for you." Ever since then, I have tried to listen in silence whenever I can.

## 2. Christmas Eve  (12-24-2008)

Fletcher and Rev. Kristi came for Christmas Eve dinner. Again, I ordered a turkey dinner from King Soopers. I asked Kristi to pray for us before the meal. We had a great time. I was glad they both came and shared their lives with me. I heard that when you love your loved ones, the first Holiday is the hardest. Because God brought healing in me, I did not get sad. I wasn't focusing on Keith. I thanked God for my son and friend who came to have a meal with me.

## 3. Christmas Day  (12-25-2008)

Fletcher came and had dinner with me. It was a peaceful day.

I organized a special Christmas program for the women at the facility. I was thankful Angela and Kristi came and helped me.

## 4. The Good-Bye Letter (12-26-2008)

This morning, God asked me to write a good-bye letter to Keith. I did not understand why I had to do it since I was healed from grief and loss. I figured that God has a reason for it, so I wrote a good-bye letter to him:

Dearest Keith,

Our Lord is amazing and loving. He has so much compassion to guide me in my grieving process. He answered so many people's prayers, and prayers of mine as well as yours. God brought healing from the grief when I lost you. I had to pray to let you go since that was hindering my healing process. If I truly believe that you are in heaven with Jesus, I shouldn't grieve, but rejoice. I was grieving, and God confronted me on that and helped me to change my heart, so I can let you go. By the time I moved into my new home, God freed me from sorrow and pain. It's a miracle. He brought healing to my mind and heart. I plan to write a book on how God has brought healing in me. It's God's grace that I am writing this without breaking down in tears. I am thankful that He has directed and guided me in my grieving process.

Even now, God asked me to write this good-bye letter to you. It has been six months since you left this earth and have gone to the Lord. He has healed me from losing you. I write this with great affection and love for you, knowing that you will be a great servant to God in heaven and give Him glory in every way. I will try to do the same as long as I live. I made a decision to love the Lord. That is my first priority. I will be depending on God to lead my ministry. I am so blessed. I am thankful God has been leading me in my walk and teaching me how to focus on Him, plus how to love and serve Jesus. I am grateful that you helped me in my preparation for ministry. I thank you for that. You typed all my papers when I attended Multnomah Bible College. I only typed one last paper before I graduated. God told me that you helped me in my ministry preparation process more than anyone, and I know it is true.

I am sorry I was not able to take you out for dinner

after I received a check from the Upper Room for a weekly devotion which I wrote. I thank God for you and thank you for trying to be a good husband, even in our challenging situations and difficult times with our children. You were a good husband. I couldn't have asked for anyone better. If we were to live again, I would marry you again because I love you so much more than anyone else I have ever met.

You brought so much healing in my heart and challenged me to grow in faith. You also prepared me for the challenges of everyday life by pushing me to be independent in every way. I thank you for that, and thank you for everything you have done to make me happy with your creativity and humor. I say good-bye to you because I can't hold on to you anymore. God teaches me that I have to give Him everything that concerns me, including you, so I can devote myself to loving God and helping others who are hurting and are in need of my care. Among them are our beautiful children, our families, and our friends who are still grieving the loss of you. I need to be a mom and a dad because you cannot take care of our children anymore. Pray for me for God's wisdom, knowledge, understanding and revelation, so I can guide our children to help them to experience God's love, power, and healing. Until I see you again, Good-bye and take care of God's business in heaven as I do here on earth as long as God will allow me. Thank you again for your love. Pray for me, our children, and our family and friends. I love you.

Your wife forever,

Yong Hui

## 5. My Beautiful Daughter  (12-29-2008)
I went to work, but I did not feel like I wanted to lead worship because I wanted to visit my daughter. I called some volunteers, but I couldn't make arrangements, and I canceled the worship services. I left and drove 400 miles to my daughter's home in Buffalo.

I enjoyed the drive. When I was grieving, driving was a trigger and brought pain, but since God healed me, I can focus on driving. I enjoyed the beautiful mountains, fields, clouds, and blue sky. God gave me a deep sense of the beauty of nature. God can create so much beauty with just words, and He shares the beauty with us by giving us the sense to understand and feel the beauty. This is the first time I have driven to

Buffalo by myself since Keith died. I enjoyed the silence, and my heart was filled with gratitude, joy, and peace. I first thought that going to Buffalo by myself would be difficult, but I enjoyed it because I like to be alone. Whenever I am alone, God's presence is so real.

When I arrived in Buffalo, I drove to the bowling alley because on Monday nights my daughter bowls with her mother-in-law and sister -in-law. I watched Nicole bowl. I was thankful that I was able to do that. I was my daughter's cheerleader there. Nicole has been a wonderful daughter. She has always had the gift of understanding others' pain, even when she was little. Since she was 15 years old, she has worked and has been financially independent. The restaurant where she worked gave her left over buffet food, and our family really enjoyed the food. One day my good friend and spiritual mentor, Patty, was having problems. Her husband, Frank, flew from Glasgow to Denver Veteran's Hospital. I decided to go to Denver and Nicole handed me $20 for my trip. I did not ask her, but she thought I needed it. That touched me deeply. She always has been perceptive and compassionate. I thank God that He blessed her with a wonderful husband and their three beautiful daughters.

When I went to Nicole's home, Teila and Jamie gave me such long, nice hugs. They are more like my little angels. When I am with them, I feel like I am in heaven. God blessed me through my family.

## 6. My Regrets  (12-30-2008)

One of my regrets in raising my children is this: while they were growing up, I did not teach them how to help the poor and those who are hurting. We were poor and struggled to survive financially. That did not leave much room for us to think about others who were in need of our care. In addition, I was ignorant about others' suffering and did not know how to look beyond my own needs. I am thankful that Fletcher was able to go on mission trips to Mexico for two months and to South Korea for six months.

I talked to Nicole about how I had suffered from different triggers because of Keith's death and how God had brought healing in me. While I was sharing, I was choked with tears and Nicole was also in tears. I wanted her to know that God healed my grieving heart, and she doesn't have to worry about me anymore.

## 7. Grandpa, Keith's Prayer  (12-31-2008)

I had a dream that I gave a presentation to a group, and I was ready to give another. In the meantime, there was a distraction, and people were kept waiting. After I woke up from this dream, I made a decision to speed up the Spanish book project. I am still waiting for editing to be done on two books, but I need to focus on this project and send it to the publisher. I made a goal to send them to the publisher by the end of February 2009. TPPM is trying to raise $16,000 to distribute 10,000 copies each of *Journey With Jesus* and *Maximum Saints: Ordained by God*, to jails and prisons in America. We received a $10,000 grant from the General Board of Higher Education and Ministry for this Spanish book project. I have no doubt that all of the funding will come, because God is leading this project.

I got up early and worked on my book, *Dancing in the Sky*. I cried many times. I know the Holy Spirit will use this book to bring healing to many.

Teila woke up, so I shared the book, *Journey with Jesus* with her. I showed her the illustrations by Charles Poke, a former inmate artist at ACDF. I explained to her how Jesus walked with me and helped me. I asked her if she knew any prayers. She said she didn't. I asked her if she knew the Lord's Prayer and then started reciting it. She said, "That's Grandpa Keith's prayer." I was filled with gratitude and respect for my husband. He used to sit with Teila and work on his laptop computer. He must have tried to teach her the Lord's Prayer.

One day, Jamie's hands were on top of Teila's head and Keith said, "Look, Jamie is baptizing Teila. She is going to be a minister." We all laughed at that. "Lord, thank you for Keith's love for our family and our grandchildren."

I slept in Teila and Jamie's room, and I prayed the Lord's Prayer for them. Nicole came in and sang, "You Are My Sunshine." She sang this song for Teila and then Jamie. I was touched that Nicole was giving individual attention to her kids. This also reminded me of what I did when Nicole was little. I used to sing to her before she went to sleep. Nicole is a great mom. I am so proud of her.

## 8. Valuing Him  (1-4-2009)

This morning I asked the Lord what He wants to speak to me. He asked me not to get busy, but wait and listen. Thirty-one years ago, Keith and I met at Pastor's Kim's home, and we decided to get married. I asked, "Was it worth it?" My answer was, "Yes, it was worth it. Keith was worth it. I loved him more than anyone else I have met." This evening, God spoke to me, "My daughter, I am always with you. You don't need to feel lonely." I don't feel lonely when I am with God.

## 9. The Price  (1-5-2009)

This morning, I asked the Lord what I should sing for him. He gave me a song. I felt so much love for Jesus that tears streamed down my cheeks as I sang for Him.

I cried a lot while I was working on the book, _Dancing in the Sky_. When I feel the presence of the anointing Holy Spirit, lots of times tears come. I feel I need to get this book out as soon as possible to tell the world how God healed my grief. By sharing the story, I will be a cheerleader for Jesus.

I realize that my house is a house of prayer. I enjoy the silence and enjoy being alone with God. I have everything I need. I focus on loving God, listening to Bible tapes, praying, working on the book project, and focusing on ministry.

When I was grieving the loss of Keith, I thought I would be grieving until I died. I thank God for His grace and bringing me out of pain and suffering. I was filled with joy after I heard how much this book was helping the inmates who were editing it. I said, "Keith, you paid the great price for the book. Without you, there would be no such book as _Dancing in the Sky_."

I have to give God credit for this book. Without his healing power, I couldn't have started to write this book. I did not plan to write this book, but God planned it as He had told me. "Thank you, Lord Jesus, for leading my life. You blessed me in my spiritual journey more than I can imagine."

I asked the Lord to give me confirmation that this book will help others. I had no doubt about it, but I wanted to hear from the Lord. I sometimes ask the Lord for confirmation in different matters.

In 2008, I had asked for confirmation that He would provide all the funding for the _Maximum Saints_ books. I was sending it to the publisher, but we were short $2,000. God already told me He would provide all the funding, but I prayed, "Lord, I want confirmation from you that you will provide all the funding today." That day, a Korean woman that I had never met called me and told me that she would like to donate for TPPM project. She told me she saw my prison ministry article in the Christian Home Korean Newspaper a while back, and that day she decided to call me to let me know that she would like to help me with the funding. She didn't donate all the funds that day but her call was a confirmation from the Lord. God provided all the funding.

## 10. The Last Words  (1-7-2009)

In a dream, Keith was serving a master. I believe this master was Jesus. When Keith saw me he came and gently lifted me up to the high ceiling and while he was putting me down I said, "I love you more than anyone else I have ever met. Do you know that?" Keith was so touched; he embraced me tightly with affection. I felt his love, and then I woke up. Interestingly, Keith looked much younger and was taller than when he was alive. God gave me an understanding that He gave me the chance to say my last words to Keith. This made me cry. I was filled with gratitude. "Lord Jesus, I love you. I just don't have enough words to say it. You know my heart. I wanted to say my last words to him. Thank you for giving me the opportunity to tell him that I love him." I asked the Lord which song I should sing for Him. He gave me a song, "My Life Flows Rich in Love and Grace," and I sang for Him in tears.

In 2008 on Valentine's Day, I gave Keith a candle holder. It had paintings of hearts with roses and the words: "The One I love, if I could choose again, I'd still choose you." Keith was happy when he received it.

I prayed for others who are affected by Keith's death. I did not realize this earlier, but there are so many who are grieving. As a pastor, Keith served eight churches altogether for the last 21 years. I prayed, "Lord, please heal everyone who is mourning the loss of Keith. Please have mercy on them and heal them as you have healed me."

## 11. A House of Prayer (1-9-2009)

I will be flying to Orlando, Florida, to attend the American Correctional Chaplain's Association (ACCA) meeting and to go before the board for an interview to be a certified chaplain.

Yolanda will come and stay two days to pray in my home while I am gone. That really makes me happy, because my house will be a house of prayer. She will be the first one to use my guest room to pray. Thank you, God. She has blessed me so much.

## 12. ACCA Interview (1-10-2009)

The ACCA interview team was amazed by what the ACDF program department was doing to help the inmates through TPPM books and DVDs. They told me that was unheard of. There were no other facilities in the USA where inmates write stories to help other inmates. Moreover, the books and DVDs are distributed to jails, prisons, and homeless shelters nationwide, free of charge. They praised the ACDF program department's creativity. Other chaplains viewed the books and DVDs and were inspired by them. I received many requests for books from many chaplains in different states. I was very happy and encouraged.

I am very thankful for Program Coordinator Mr. Sterritt Fuller at ACDF. He supports what I am trying to accomplish. My goal is to help people to experience transformation in their hearts so their lives can be transformed in a positive way. There is no transformation of a person's behaviors without transformation of the heart. God proved to me that He has the power to help those who are open to Him and open to change. Many inmates have powerful stories of transformation and by giving them the opportunity to share their stories, others can find hope, direction, and be transformed. I am grateful that I am working in an environment where many people support what I am trying to accomplish.

### 13. Overflowing Cup (1-17-2009)

I had a visit from four Korean people whom I did not know. They took me out to lunch and donated $1,000 to the TPPM project. They said, "We do mission fundraising and we were looking to find an organization to which to donate money. Rev. Jin Tae Park, a United Methodist Minister and the editor of Christian Home Korean newspaper, gave us your name." They were happy to find out about TPPM and my prison ministry. They blessed me so much with their enthusiasm to help the prisoners. God spoke to me that I just needed to rely on Him for all of the funding, and I should not worry. "Thank you, Lord. You are really an excellent fundraiser."

### 14. Scott's Vision (1-18-2009)

I was invited to St. Paul UMC in Boulder where I showed the _Maximum Saints_ DVD introduction to the Sunday school. After that, I preached at the worship service. Scott Glancy gave a presentation on how he got involved with TPPM. Many people donated to the Transformation Project.

Scott has a Ph.D. and is a physicist. He is creative and has a big vision to help others. I told him I would like to find someone to make an animated movie from the story _Journey With Jesus_. He said, "That's pretty ambitious." I replied, "You've got to have a dream. It will help inmates who cannot read."

Scott is working on putting all the books published by TPPM on a Website, so anyone can read them. When it is finished, people from all over the world will be able to read the book without having to buy it. I would never have thought of that. I am glad that he came up with the idea. His vision was much bigger than mine. I am thrilled to see how God has brought visionaries to TPPM to make this project more successful. Our book project has to continue since prisoners do not have access to computers.

## 15. Tell Keith (1-21-2009)

I finally made arrangements with Rev. Dawnmarie to have breakfast with her in Keenesburg. It seems she has made many good changes in the churches and made progress with her two congregations. I told her that I have been working on my book, _Dancing in the Sky_. She asked me to come and share this project at her two churches. She is an encouraging and compassionate pastor. She said, "I shared your article with the administrative council about how God brought healing in you and everyone was in tears. Your visit will be good because many are still grieving. When they hear how God has brought healing, it will help them."

I will be preaching in two weeks. This will be the first time I will be back in my husband's churches since I walked out of Community UMC in tears about six months ago.

I met Karla at the church. She gave me some of Nicole's belongings she had found in the parsonage when they were cleaning. She said, "I am sorry to tell you this, but Keith's cat, Lady Midnight, died. It was a good thing that she was with us for a while. I told her many things that she could tell Keith when she finally sees him in heaven." We were both in tears. I replied, "Thank you so much for taking care of her. Keith did not want to put her to sleep when she lost bowel control, so he put her in a nursing home, a cage. I was concerned about her after Keith died. I did not want to put her to sleep and I am glad that you took care of her."

Karla said, "I believe she will be in heaven with Keith. I told her to go and tell Keith all the things I have told her. It was difficult for me to tell you about this news." I said, "A while back I had a dream that I saw a cat's arm cut off, and it looked like one of Keith's cats, but I did not want to ask anyone how the cats were doing. I was afraid that I might hear bad news. I know it's not in the Bible, but I believe all animals go to heaven since there are animals in heaven. God can do anything. I am glad that you told me about this. We will all die some day and this is a part of life. I thank you so much. Your family helped me a lot in my grieving process. You carried my burdens because I couldn't take care of Lady Midnight. Many people helped me in my grieving process, especially Keith's two congregations. It's because of many friends' prayers that I was able to experience healing so soon." Karla said, "So soon, yes, that is great."

Karla showed me the "Loaves and Fishes Food Pantry" in the education building. She said they had a lot of food because many people sent money for Keith's memorial fund.

When I went home, Rosemary came and helped me box books to send out to jails and prisons in different states. Rosemary has been helping me with labeling and packaging boxes for a long time, and her son typed addresses for me. We packed more than 15 boxes.

When we ran out of tape, I called Phil, who works in a post office. He immediately came over with more tape and helped us pack more books. Phil loaded all the boxes in his truck. I met him at the post office and mailed them. Phil has been helping me with shipping and distributing books whenever TPPM receives them, two pallets or more each time. In 2008, UPS delivered _Maximum Saints_ books three days earlier than what they had scheduled. The ACDF operator called me and said, "Chaplain, you are receiving a big load." I knew then I had to make quick arrangements. I flipped through volunteer names and Phil's name came up. I didn't know who he was, but I called him and explained to him that the Transformation Project received more than 100 boxes of books, and I needed someone with a truck to help me clear the loading dock. Within five minutes, Phil showed up and loaded the books in his truck, took them to the post office. I mailed them to different states with his help. After that, he made many more trips to the storage garage, so we could mail more books later.

Since then, Phil helps me whenever I receive big loads of books. It's God's grace that Rosemary and Phil could help me with the book project to help the incarcerated. I am blessed to know many wonderful people through the TPPM because without them, I wouldn't be able to do all the work. _"Just as each of us has one body with many members, and these members do not all have the same function, so in Christ we who are many form one body, and each member belongs to all the others. We have different gifts, according to the grace given us."_ (Romans 12:4-6a)

16. Encouraging Letter (1-22-2009)

The Holy Spirit gave me a song when I woke up this morning, "Come to me, come to me, those who are grieving and sad." My heart became filled with anticipation and excitement to work on the book, _Dancing in the Sky_. This joy I am feeling is from the Holy Spirit. I couldn't be happier.

God gave me confirmation about this book project through Ana, one of the saints in our facility. She has been editing this book. This is what she wrote:

<u>A letter written by Ana</u>

I was led by the Holy Spirit to write this letter to you after reading your testimony and letter about the loss of your husband. But before I go on, I'd like to let you know that I was unaware of your loss until now. I give you my utmost respect and condolence on your loss.

Your testimony has opened up my eyes, heart, soul, and mind for everything the Lord has lined up for me. I lost my mother due to cancer. On February 27, 2009, it will be seven years. It was the day before my birthday. I was a lost cause. I did not want to hear from anybody, being rebellious to all. Speaking for myself, I hung on to the past life I had lived and was also hanging on to my Mom's death. I wasn't accepting it. Your testimony and your good-bye letter to your husband seemed to me to be closure. Closure is something I did not have.

Thank you for your encouraging words and insights of what you have gone through and the tests you have passed. You are right about one thing: without God we cannot do anything. Through this I understand now why God sent me here and why He has placed me in your path. Through you, in everything you have done, written and spoken, God is showing me how to overcome my depression, oppression, deceit, anger, condemnation, crack, and prostitution. I believe in my heart there are no more chances. Through you, the Lord has strengthened me, taught me, and set me free. In all, He has prepared me and shown me what He expects, but He gives me that choice of life or death, blessings or curses. Today I choose life and blessings in Jesus' name. Now my Mom can be happy to see me from heaven, walking with the Lord like she has always wanted me to do.

Chaplain McDonald, your many words, prayers, worship services, and praise for the Lord have inspired me a lot to keep pressing forward and not to dwell on past sin and losses of life. My higher power has always lighted my path to walk on and has shown me and given me a way out of nowhere. His grace is sufficient for me. It's not so much the fall that counts, but to pick myself up and to keep on moving forward.

2 Corinthians 2:10-16 is the highlight of my life on a daily basis. I know I have read it plenty of times but today it sinks in and penetrates throughout my whole body, which is of Christ.

Prayer: "Father God, thank you for giving me life and for living in me. Thank you for forgiveness and for setting me free from the past. I thank you, Lord, for Chaplain McDonald and using her as a vessel to strengthen others through her powerful testimonies.

Thank you, Lord, for your grace, mercy, and your unconditional love. Lord, without you I could not pass the daily challenges if I did not acknowledge you through my trials and tribulations. Thank you for your wisdom, and because of you, my love and faith in you have grown. Thank you for setting me free from grief, and giving me strength to give my mother to you and letting her go.

Thank you, Lord, for acknowledging me, loving me, and giving me chance after chance when I don't deserve it. Lord, I ask in your son Jesus' name to continue to hold on to me and put your eyes and feet on me to be able to see and walk with you daily. In Jesus' name I pray. Your will be done. Amen."

After I read Ana's letter, I was deeply touched. "Thank you Lord, Jesus, for Ana's encouraging letter. Use this book to bring healing, especially to those who are grieving. Lord, I give you my tears if that will bring healing in others. I give you everything I have for your glory. Your love and power brought healing in my heart. I pray that your power will continuously work with grieving hearts, so people will not be paralyzed with pain and grief, but filled with joy. They can tell the world that you are alive, you care, and you have the power to heal! You have done it with me, Lord. I can give you thanks and praise instead of grieving the loss. I love you, Lord Jesus. You blessed me so much and thank you for helping me to recognize this. Thank you for many friends who have helped me in my grieving process. I even thank you for my tears and pain, because you helped me to experience your love and healing power. It's your grace that brought me out of pain and grief. I pray this in your glorious name, Jesus. Amen."

I've never seen Ana that happy. She was glowing and I could say she truly had experienced healing from the loss of her mother.

God gave me a vision of a little girl wearing a white dress giving flowers to Jesus. That girl is me. God is showing me that my love for the Lord Jesus is like giving Him flowers to make Him happy. I thank God for this vision. All I can say these days is, "Lord Jesus, I am so happy with you. I am in love with you."

### 17. Spanish Book Project (1-22-2009)

Today I received an e-mail from Rocky Mountain Conference Spanish Ministry Initiative stating that TPPM will be receiving $4,000 for the Spanish book project. That made me so happy. We only need to raise $2,000 more. The ACDF inmates are almost finished with proofreading, so I plan to send it to the publisher no later than the end of February 2009. "Lord, you are great. You know what we need. Bless this book project. So many people will be saved and find peace, encouragement, and hope in you."

Six bi-lingual inmates from F 1200 are editing the Spanish book project, and it is a blessing to see how they are eager to help other inmates with this project. The vision for this Spanish book project came from ACDF inmate leaders who wanted to see *Journey With Jesus* in Spanish. Four bi-lingual inmates translated the whole book, and now, in addition to *Journey With Jesus, Maximum Saints Ordained By God* is going to be published in Spanish.

### 18. Stories of Tears (1-29-2009)

While I was leading worship in A Module, God gave me a vision. Jesus was about to give me a paper, and his tears dropped to the paper; the tears became written words. He said, "Stories written with tears bring healing." I was in tears. This book was necessary because I have experienced an unexpected miraculous healing from the Lord, and I cannot hide it. It is written with tears and the Lord knows it. I know the anointing of the Holy Spirit was with me when I was writing. *"Those who sow in tears will reap with songs of joy. He who goes out weeping, carrying seed to sow, will return with songs of joy, carrying sheaves with him." (Psalm 126:5)*

Many are still grieving the loss of Keith. I wanted them to know that God can bring healing in their hearts like He has healed me. "I thank you, God, for your guidance in writing this book. You blessed me so much through my loss of Keith because you have taught me that our spirit will live even though our physical body dies. You will wipe our tears, there will be no pain and suffering because of your power to make a new heavenly home for us. Thank you, Jesus, for your love and power. Let me love you, Lord Jesus, and my love and commitment to serve you will be pleasing to you. Amen."

*A Story of Hope for Grieving Hearts*                                    101

## 19. God the Fundraiser (2-1-2009)

I shared my testimonial sermons at the two churches that Keith served before he died. God blessed me while I was sharing the testimony. Many people came to me after the service and told me that my story brought healing in their hearts.

I visited Deputy Duran, and after a while she told me she had thought about sending funds for the Transformation Project the whole time she was talking with me. I had to laugh. I told her my gift must be fundraising. While we were in Plains, Montana, I visited my good friend Elva. As soon as she saw me, she opened her purse and took out her wallet and said, "Yong Hui, what is that project on which you are working? I wanted to give you the money for your project." I said, "I came here to visit you, not to collect your money. If you want to donate, you can donate to the church."

At that time, I was doing three fundraisers: The first one was called, "King's Closet", which was helping pastors' families who did not have enough money to buy food. The second one was to help the Sunday school. The third one was to help raise money for a bathroom for the Paradise UMC that only had an outhouse.

Last year, Keith and I were at the Lunch Bunch senior lunch in Keenesburg. One woman I knew fell hard on the hardwood floor, and everyone was very quiet. Then two ladies slowly helped her stand up. While she was getting up, she saw me and she blurted out, "Yong Hui, I need to send you the money for your project. I need to know where to send the money." I gave her the Transformation Project brochure so she could send the money.

I have many stories like this. I don't usually ask people for money for the book project, but when I share about what I am doing, people volunteer to give. God has blesses me with other people's generosity. I just can't believe what God can do.

I know where these people's thoughts originated. The Holy Spirit reminds them to donate because they need to give. That has happened to me many times. God was teaching me to be generous. When God asked me to give, He would be specific about it. He would tell me when, how much, and to whom. That's why when people ask me how much they should donate for TPPM, I tell them to ask God. God has been teaching me not to rely on material things but on Him. This experience with Deputy Duran encouraged me. I was concerned about how I could raise funds for this book. God has a sense of humor when it comes to fundraising. He told me if I worry about the funds, I am trying to do His job. He was right. I try to do my part and share this project continuously with others so they can have more opportunities to give, and I know the Holy Spirit leads this project.

Since _Dancing in the Sky_ book is related to my husband's death and my own grieving story, I decided to raise funds apart from TPPM fundraising. God has been challenging me to enlarge my vision with this project. I plan to print 10,000 and God asked me what would I do if I raised more money than I need. I had to think for a while to answer Him, then an idea came to me. We hardly have any Spanish inspirational books. I would like to have it translated. This will help many Hispanics who are grieving. After I made that decision, I thought there was no reason to wait. Even though I am still working on fundraising for the English book, I decided to start the translation.

I asked Juanito Max Milanes in F1200 to help me find bi-lingual inmates to translate this book. Previously, he had organized the translation and editing of two Spanish books. Mr. Milanes has read the book. He told me it helped his grieving process. He lost family members. F1200 inmates have started translating the book. I have confidence that the Lord will provide all the funding. My faith keeps growing as I try to listen to the Holy Spirit and obey Him. God certainly has a way of changing my little plans to big plans: help prisoners who cannot voice their needs.

This year many good things happened with TPPM production. Michael Goins produced a DVD called, _Maximum Saints Walk into the Light_, which had Timothy Garcia and Lonnie Griego's powerful transformation stories to help the younger generation. 1,000 copies of the DVD will be ready to distribute to jails, prisons, and homeless shelters within a month. We also plan to send it free of charge to outside churches, organizations and youth groups to warn them of the danger of drugs, alcohol, and violence.

20. Kindness and Healing  (2-2-2009)

I happened to be at the headquarters of the Sheriff's Administrative office, and I asked the clerk if Lt. David Shipley was there. She said, "He is with someone, and his office door is closed, but I can go and tell him that you are here." I replied, "No, you don't need to bother him." She said, "Oh, no, it's not a problem. He told me whenever you want to talk to him, I can interrupt anytime." I said, "No, I don't need to talk to him right now." I left. Lt. Shipley told me if I stop to talk to him at anytime; he would listen to me. I did not realize that he also told the clerk the same thing. I felt encouraged to know that God placed many wonderful Christians in my path to show kindness and care. This brings healing in my heart. I also have met many deputies who showed so much concern for me after Keith died. One deputy said, "After your husband died, we were all just quiet because we did not know what to say." I responded, "God is great! He brought healing in me that I can smile and thank God for everything." Another deputy was telling me that he was having a difficult time. I asked, "More than me?" He replied, "Oh, no, I don't have any problems." Moreover, my story of healing brought healing in many inmates' hearts as well. I thank God for that.

### 21. Loving Jesus (2-3-2009)
The Holy Spirit woke me up with a song: "I want to know you... You are my all, my joy, my righteousness, and I love you, Lord." I read Paul's letter: *"But whatever was to my profit I now consider loss for the sake of Christ. What is more, I consider everything a loss compared to the surpassing greatness of knowing Christ Jesus my Lord, for whose sake I have lost all things. I consider them rubbish, that I may gain Christ and be found in him, not having a righteousness of my own that comes from the law, but that which is through faith in Christ-- the righteousness that comes from God and is by faith. I want to know Christ and the power of his resurrection and the fellowship of sharing in his sufferings, becoming like him in his death, and so, somehow, to attain to the resurrection from the dead. Not that I have already obtained all this, or have already been made perfect, but I press on to take hold of that for which Christ Jesus took hold of me. Brothers, I do not consider myself yet to have taken hold of it. But one thing I do: Forgetting what is behind and straining toward what is ahead, I press on toward the goal to win the prize for which God has called me heavenward in Christ Jesus." (Philippians 3:7-14)*

Paul's commitment to knowing Christ encouraged me so much. If I can focus on knowing Jesus, I will be able to love Him as I should. "Lord Jesus, I love you more than anyone, and more than anything. I cannot help but to tell the world that you have so much love, compassion, and power to heal. Now, I understand why I am called to be your cheerleader. I am so happy with you. I am in love with you, Lord Jesus."

Note: *Dancing in the Sky, A Story of Hope for Grieving Heart* book was published in May 2009, ten months after Keith's death and the DVD, *Dancing in the Sky, Mismatched Shoes* was produced in December 2009, 18 months after my husband's death. That's God's grace.

## Part Two: Yong Hui's Message to
## Keith's Two Last Congregations

Feb. 1, 2009 - I shared the following testimonial sermon at Community United Methodist Church in Keenesburg and James Memorial United Methodist Church in Hudson, where Keith served as a pastor before he passed away. My intention was to help the grieving congregations to experience healing from the loss of Keith. Rev. Dawnmarie is their new pastor, and she invited me to come and share my journey of grief and healing. After the service, I received many encouraging comments and many told me that my sharing brought healing to their hearts. Later, this message was sent to six more congregations that Keith had served during his 21 years of ministry.

### *"Dancing in the Sky"*

Scripture: *"Jesus said to her, 'I am the resurrection and the life. He who believes in me will live, even though he dies; and whoever lives and believes in me will never die. Do you believe this?'" (John 11:25-26)*

I am here today because of all your support in my grief and healing process and I wanted to share how God brought healing to my heart from the loss of Keith.

I thank you for helping me when I was going through a very difficult time. Many of you helped me with prayers, food, cleaning, hauling out garbage, writing thank you notes, moving, and so much more that I cannot mention everything. I especially thank Rev. Dawnmarie, who has helped me a lot in my grieving process.

You helped me a lot in my healing process, and God helped me step by step in my grieving process and brought healing. I will share how He did these wonders in my life.

*A Story of Hope for Grieving Hearts* 105

July 9, 2008, was my day off and I was home doing chores. Around noon, Keith asked me to take pictures of him riding his recumbent bike to add to his email devotion.

I took many pictures of him. That evening we were invited to a Special Olympics dinner at Adams County Fairgrounds at 6:30 p.m. Keith told me he would be done with Tae Kwon Do class at 5:30 p.m. I had been asked to pray before the meal. I had an uneasy feeling that if we went together I might be late, so we decided to drive separately. I left home early and went to the Adams County Fairgrounds.

Keith did not get there by the time the dinner started. I called him on his cell phone, but he did not answer. He never showed up and I thought he finished Tae Kwon Do so late that he decided not to come.

By the time I left the Fairgrounds it was about 8:30 p.m. and while I was passing Hwy 85 and 144th Ave., I saw two police cars with their lights flashing. There was an accident.

When I got home, there was a police car parked in front of our home. The police told me that Keith was in a car accident and transported to Denver Health that morning. I told them they had the wrong person because Keith was home that afternoon. They checked his name and told me it was Keith.

I thought Keith was in a minor car accident since he was never in an accident during our 30 years of marriage. Then the police officer got a call and said to me that Keith had died. I couldn't believe it. Helen came with her son and took me to the hospital, and Jody and David came for support.

From then on, I was immersed in grief. We were planning to go to Montana for the McDonald's family reunion on July 17, and July 17 ended up being Keith's funeral.

I was immobilized with so much grief and pain that I couldn't work. There are many ways God brought healing, and the first day Keith died, God told me my husband lived a full life. He helped me to accept Keith's death even though I did not understand it.

Then three days after he died, I asked the Lord to show me that He was taking care of Keith. That night, I had a dream and in the dream Keith came and bowed to me and said, "Thank you." Then he disappeared. That brought so much healing.

One Sunday, I visited James Memorial UMC, and then when I went to attend First Community UMC, I was so overwhelmed with grief that I couldn't even stay to worship and left in tears. I went home and asked God for the first time, "Why do I have to go through this?"

Still, I wasn't able to go back to work because I was in so much pain. After three weeks, I went to lead worship at ACDF, but I walked out of there in tears. I was glad that I had an intern that day to lead worship for me.

I was incapable of doing anything with ministry or the book projects. So, Fletcher and I went to visit my daughter for four days. After we came back, I dropped off Fletcher at his apartment. While I was driving, I was listening to the song, "God of Wonders," which was one of Keith's favorite songs. Suddenly, I had a vision of Keith dancing in the sky with a big smile and making a big circle. I couldn't believe it. I was so happy to see him and thanked God for the vision.

I wanted to take dancing lessons with Keith when he was alive. He told me he couldn't dance, and he did not want to take lessons. God has a sense of humor to show me Keith dancing so well and with a happy smile.

This vision brought so much healing. I thought if Keith is happy in heaven, I should be happy. I was able to go back to work the next day, and started sharing my story of how God brought healing in my grieving heart.

Still, I was only functioning at 50 percent and I had to go through so much mourning and grieving because healing is a process. I cried for two days while I was packing Keith's books. I cried when I packed up Keith's clothes and cleaned his bathroom.

From then on, I suffered from triggers that caused me to grieve. Everything could become a trigger, and I would break down. When I saw a man who looked like Keith, or saw a red truck, it was a trigger. When I saw a couple walking together, it was a trigger. Keith's birthday was a trigger. Coming back to an empty home was a trigger. Any of Keith's friends could be a trigger. Driving was a trigger.

One day I was crying because I thought about how much pain Keith was in when he got hit by a car. That almost immobilized my thinking process, and I turned left on a red light. I barely missed an oncoming car. Keith died when he was turning left and was hit by an oncoming car. I did not know how to be healed from grieving. If it was up to me, I wouldn't have been healed. I made plans to grieve until I died because I had lost the person that I loved the most.

One day, I asked the Lord if there was anything that He wanted to tell me. He told me He could heal my broken heart, but I was not willing to let my husband go. He reminded me of my aunt who prayed to God to take away all of her thoughts about her deceased husband. God healed her. She did not grieve anymore.

The day I closed the house, God told me not to bring Keith to my new home. God was preparing a new journey for me, but I was not willing. I didn't even go into the new home the day I closed because I was not willing to let my husband go. Finally, I realized that I cannot grieve anymore because it was so painful, and also God was after me. I was praying to God to heal my broken heart.

Then God gave me a vision that I was tightly holding a clear plastic balloon shaped like my husband, and Jesus was standing by the door of my new house, waiting for me. Jesus was ready to lead me into the next stage of my life, but I wasn't ready to follow Him. God confronted me with my distraction from my spiritual journey with Him because of my grieving. Then I knew that I had to let go of all my plans to grieve for Keith.

If I truly believed that Keith was happy in heaven with Jesus, I should not grieve. I prayed, "God, I give all my desires, wishes, self-pity, regrets, dreams, and everything associated with my husband to you. Please take away any thoughts associated with Keith and heal my grieving heart." I was able to move into my new home after that.

Since then, God worked a miracle. I haven't had any

triggers and I don't grieve any more. I haven't broken down, not even once, because I miss Keith. God took away that desire as well. Now, I just have good memories of Keith and can smile and enjoy my life. Of course, I cry at times when I share my pain and grief and what I have gone through in this journey of loss. Now, I rejoice that God has brought healing in my heart.

Since God healed me, I was able to work on my book project for the Transformation Project. Also, I started writing a book, _Dancing in the Sky_. I plan to publish 10,000 copies of this book by the end of May 2009. I will distribute them to people who knew Keith and to jails, prisons and homeless shelters throughout the United States to help those who are grieving from the loss of their loved ones.

Healing is a process, and God is still working with me in many areas. On December 26, God asked me to write a good-bye letter to Keith. Here is the letter:

Dearest Keith,

Our Lord is amazing and loving. He has so much compassion to guide me in my grieving process. He answered so many people's prayers, and prayers of mine as well as yours. God brought healing from the grief when I lost you. I had to pray to let you go since that was hindering my healing process. If I truly believe that you are in heaven with Jesus, I shouldn't grieve, but rejoice. I was grieving, and God confronted me on that and helped me to change my heart, so I can let you go. By the time I moved into my new home, God freed me from sorrow and pain. It's a miracle. He brought healing to my mind and heart. I plan to write a book on how God has brought healing in me. It's God's grace that I am writing this without breaking down in tears. I am thankful that He has directed and guided me in my grieving process.

Even now, God asked me to write this good-bye letter to you. It has been six months since you left this earth and have gone to the Lord. He has healed me from losing you. I write this with great affection and love for you, knowing that you will be a great servant to God in heaven and give Him glory in every way. I will try to do the same as long as I live. I made a decision to love the Lord. That is my first priority. I will be depending on God to lead my ministry. I am so blessed. I am thankful God has been leading me in my walk and teaching me how to focus on Him, plus how to love and serve Jesus.

I am grateful that you helped me in my preparation for ministry. I thank you for that. You typed all my papers when I attended Multnomah Bible College. I only typed one last paper before I graduated. God told me that you helped me in my ministry preparation process more than anyone, and I know it is true.

I am sorry I was not able to take you out for dinner after I received a check from the Upper Room for a weekly devotion which I wrote. I thank God for you and thank you for trying to be a good husband, even in our challenging situations and difficult times with our children. You were a good husband. I couldn't have asked for anyone better. If we were to live again, I would marry you again because I love you so much more than anyone else I have ever met.

You brought so much healing in my heart and challenged me to grow in faith. You also prepared me for the challenges of everyday life by pushing me to be independent in every way. I thank you for that, and thank you for everything you have done to make me happy with your creativity and humor. I say good-bye to you because I can't hold on to you anymore. God teaches me that I have to give Him everything that concerns me, including you, so I can devote myself to loving God and helping others who are hurting and are in need of my care. Among them are our beautiful children, our families, and our friends who are still grieving the loss of you. I need to be a mom and a dad because you cannot take care of our children anymore. Pray for me for God's wisdom, knowledge, understanding and revelation, so I can guide our children to help them to experience God's love, power, and healing. Until I see you again, Good-bye and take care of God's business in heaven

*Dancing in the Sky*

as I do here on earth as long as God will allow me. Thank you again for your love. Pray for me, our children, and our family and friends. I love you.

Your wife forever,

Yong Hui

These days, I say, "Jesus, I am so happy with you. I'm in love with you." I couldn't say that when I was grieving, but now I can. God blessed me so much. One of the blessings happened through a dream not long ago. In this dream, Keith was serving a master. I believe this master is Jesus. When Keith saw me he came and gently lifted me up to the high ceiling and while he was putting me down, I said, "I love you more than anyone else I have ever met. Do you know that?" Keith was so touched; he embraced me tightly with affection. I felt his love and then I woke up. Interestingly, Keith looked much younger than his age. He did not have any wrinkles and he was tall. Fletcher and I talked about how people look young in heaven. We laughed because if people are much younger looking than their age in heaven, Keith might have much more hair on his head.

God gave me an understanding that He gave me the chance to tell Keith my last words to him, which I wasn't able to do before he died. I can tell the world that God has so much love and power to heal our broken hearts. I know many of you are grieving because of the loss of Keith. It's time to give him to God so that we will be able to focus on loving God and helping others who are hurting.

My story of healing is a blessing from God, and I need to tell others about what God can do. That's why I am working on my book, _Dancing in the Sky_. God blessed me so much with this book already, and many inmates who are editing it have experienced healing. That's God's grace.

Thank you for giving me the chance to share my testimony. Thank you for carrying my burdens when I needed help the most. God bless you. Let us pray that God will bring healing in the areas that need healing.

## Part Three: Keith's Last Email Devotion
### Written on July 9, 2008

Keith was not able to send out this email devotion he wrote because he died that night, but our daughter, Nicole, sent it out to others.

### *"Finding Roadside Treasure"*

I recently got a new bicycle, a *Cruzbike* recumbent bike with a sort of chair-like seat instead of the terribly uncomfortable saddle on regular upright bikes. Because of the way you sit, kind of leaning back a bit, it's easier to breathe and much easier on the shoulders and neck muscles. Better for sightseeing than traditional road bikes where you're all hunched over and having to crane your neck to see where you're going. And it has less wind resistance which means more speed! Aargh! Aargh! Aargh! On the downside, it's taken some getting used to because the balance is different than an upright bike, but I'm getting the hang of it. I hardly fall down at all lately, not even at stop signs when I get started up. Graveled roads, though, are still a challenge.

As I ride around I look for and pick up roadside treasures, mostly things that have fallen off vehicles: an American flag, a Jackson Lake Competition '93 banner, a 3/8" open end and box end wrench, T-shirts, cargo straps, webbing, sunglasses, to mention a few of the treasures I've collected out there. I keep looking for that suitcase full of money, but so far I haven't spotted it. I'll let you know if I do.

Riding around and looking for roadside treasures is a metaphor for life, a parable about traveling on the Christian path. Some people might ride the roads or drive the highways and never even notice the roadside treasures that are there. Zoom! Zoom! As they rush to get where they're going, they miss out on the beauty of the journey itself and the various blessings that await us around the bends and turns of life.

Others might notice some of the roadside treasures but are too busy to stop to investigate or take advantage of the free gifts that are out there along the road. Maybe they're not motivated enough to stop and pick stuff up. Or for some other reasons they just miss out on things along the path they're traveling. But some do stop and pick up the roadside treasures. Some of the stuff might not be in such good shape, but some is quite serviceable. And some in brand new condition. Free stuff just for the taking. Roadside treasures. Free gifts.

What kind of person are you? Do you take advantage of the roadside treasures or are you too busy to stop and receive the gifts? I hope you don't miss out on the blessings from God that are scattered along the roads we travel.

I'm not really just talking about roadside treasures but about the blessings of life that we come across along the journey we're on. Sometimes it's people. Somebody shopping the same aisle as you or getting mail at the same time as you. Do you just say, "Hi." and go on with your business or do you stop and talk a bit and by your caring and cheerful attitude share the love of Jesus with that person? Just seemingly chance encounters, but, in reality, divinely designed meetings and appointments. Are you taking advantage of these God-given opportunities?

Sometimes the roadside treasures are experiences like stopping to smell the roses or look at a sunset. Or taking note of how the corn or sugar beets are growing.

Something I've really enjoyed as I've ridden around Roggen, Keenesburg, Hudson, Prospect Valley and Ft. Lupton is watching things grow. And smelling them. The flowers, the trees, the alfalfa fields. They all change each time I ride by them. It's just wonderful to get all that interesting sensory input. God has blessed us by the world around us and what's in it.

Allegorically, the roadside treasures are the Christian virtues we've been emphasizing for the past few months. Sometimes we see them in action in other people around us: appreciation, beauty, compassion, creativity, diversity, enthusiasm, flexibility, goodness, gratitude, happiness, hope, integrity, industry, joy, kindness, love, mercy, peace, reliability, self-sacrifice, wisdom, wholeheartedness, and so forth. And seeing them in others makes us want them for ourselves. How good are you at spotting those virtues in other people?

And sometimes we see those virtues in ourselves! What's growing in your life? Congeniality? Contrition? Contentment? Endurance? Faith? Forgiveness? Generosity? Holiness, humor, inquisitiveness, justice, meekness, obedience, passion, perseverance, purity, respect, selflessness, service, sincerity, or other virtues? How good are you at spotting those virtues in yourself?

In our churches I see growth happening. In our Bible studies we're growing in knowledge about the Bible and Christian living. We're growing in service and compassion as we help others around us. I see our church families growing in faith as we continue to persevere through the ups and downs of our local economy and the rough spots in the road and as we *"walk through the valley of the shadow of death" (Psalm 23:4)* through times of loss and grief and depression and sadness. We are growing as churches and individuals! Can you spot the growth?

Also, most every time I go out riding I see things that make me sad. Road kill. Dogs that have been hit by vehicles, or cats, birds, turtles. Even a snake or two.

Again, this is a parable about life. It's about the tragedies we experience. Deaths of loved ones, sickness and loss of health, the aches and pains of aging, difficulties with friends and family, financial crises. So much trouble in our world!

And as I ride I watch the watchers, the birds of prey. There's hawks, crows, blackbirds, meadowlarks, kingbirds, shrikes, all birds of prey. They're watching for mice, prairie dogs, grasshoppers and other little critters to attack and kill and destroy and eat. And some munch on road kill sometimes. Always looking for something to prey upon. Do you know people like that? Some people really are sort of predatory, hurting other people in a variety of ways. So much hurt in our world!

But there's also other kinds of watchers out there.

Mourning Doves, Eurasian Collared Doves (a relatively new immigrant to our area), and Rock Doves (or pigeons). They're reminders to me of one of our most important tasks as Christians. God calls us to be watchers and observers of the people and circumstances around us and then to pray about them. We might lament to God about the tragedies of life (Mourning Dove style: a mournful *cooo, cooo, cooo*) or we might complain to God about life or just blurt out what we think about what's going on (Eurasian Collared Dove style: *kwahk! kwahk! kwahk!*) or we might talk quietly and soothingly with God about our lives and those of our friends and neighbors (pigeon style: a gentle, calm *coo, coo, coo*). Riding has been for me an opportunity to pray along the lines of the parable thinking I've been outlining above. I try to connect stuff along the road with different kinds of prayers:

People — prayers for that person I see or for others who are on my mind
Tools and other things that fell off vehicles — the virtues of the Christian life (for myself or for others)
Fields of growing corn or alfalfa or sugar beet — the ways I'm growing as a Christian, the ways I see church people and our churches growing
Road kill — tragedies I know about, difficulties people are going through, people in the hospital
Birds of prey — problem people, trouble makers, rude people, gossips
"Peaceful" birds — prayers of lament (mourning doves), complaints to God (Eurasian collared doves), quiet "friendship" conversation (pigeons)

So not only do I get a good workout, but I've been enjoying biking as a prayer time as well, another way to live out Paul's advice for us: *"Be joyful always; pray continually; give thanks in all circumstances, for this is God's will for you in Christ Jesus." (1 Thessalonians 5:16-18)*

On the Christian Journey,

*Finding Roadside Treasure*                                        115

"C. S. Keith A. McDonald (C.S. stands for cleanly shaven. Keith shaved every Easter Sunday every year but during the winter, he had a beard.)"

Mind Scrambler for Today: According to *The Unofficial United Methodist Handbook* (2007 Abingdon Press),

Which of the following are not ways to get to know your pastor?
    a. Connect with your pastor after worship.
    b. Take your pastor to lunch after Sunday worship.
    c. Go bike riding with your pastor.
    d. Join your pastor's Tae Kwon Do club.
    e. Pray daily for your pastor, because he doesn't just work on Sunday.
    f. Ask your pastor to share with you why he entered this form of ministry.
    g. Stop by your pastor's office to talk or make an appointment to get to know him better.
    h. Invite your pastor over for an afternoon snack or dinner.
    i. Join your pastor for breakfast on Sunday mornings at the Pepper Pod restaurant.
    j. Go fishing or kayaking with your pastor.

## Part Four: A Life Story
### Written
### by Keith for His Funeral

Keith Alan McDonald was born on September 4, 1957, in Spokane, Washington, to Bernice and Desmond McDonald. The family, which included his older brother Marvin, moved to Drummond, Montana, the bull shipping capital of the world, where his father worked for the Federal Aviation Administration. It was while they lived on Wylie Avenue in the lower Rattlesnake that Keith cut his nose while playing in the woods on a camping trip.

The family moved farther up the Rattlesnake where they stayed all during Keith's growing up years. He attended Rattlesnake Grade School and graduated from Hellgate High School in 1975.

After graduating, Keith joined the United States Air Force. After basic training in San Antonio, Texas, he was sent to language school in Monterey, California, where he was trained in the Korean language to be a Voice Processing Specialist. He attended technical training school at Goodfellow Air Force Base in San Angelo, Texas, and then was sent to Osan Air Base, Korea, where he was stationed until being discharged from the Air Force in 1979, except for a summer of advanced language training at the Persidio of Monterey.

While in Korea he married Yong Hui Lee in 1978. After returning to the States, Keith and Yong Hui attended Multnomah Bible College where the motto was "If you want the Bible, you want Multnomah!" Keith graduated in 1983 with a bachelor's degree in Biblical Languages. After a semester at Western Conservative Baptist Seminary, Keith, Yong Hui, and their infant daughter Nicole and Yong Hui's mother moved to Denver, Colorado where Keith attended the Iliff School of Theology. He graduated from that seminary in 1987 with a Masters in Divinity.

His son Fletcher was born that same year.

As a probationary member of the Yellowstone Conference of the United Methodist Church, Keith was appointed to the Plains and Paradise United Methodist Churches and began his pastorate there in July 1987. Keith was a frequent contributor to the PLAINSMAN AND CLARK FORK VALLEY PRESS newspapers in a pastoral column while in Plains.

He left to serve at First Hinsdale United Methodist Church and First United Methodist Church in Glasgow, Montana, in 1992. Then he serviced First United Methodist Church in Buffalo and First United Methodist Church in Casey, Wyoming, from 1999 to 2003. He was appointed to Community United Methodist Church in Keenesburg and James Memorial United Methodist Church in Hudson in 2003.

He held concern for environmental issues and peace activism, and in the church he stressed ecumenism. His inter-religious studies included a love for Native American thought which he incorporated into his Christian lifestyle. He loved to write and wrote articles for THE SOUTH WELD SUN newspapers in the Faith section.

He viewed life as a journey of a sorts….He would like to be remembered as a prophet in the church who didn't get completely tamed by the institution, although at times he felt it was so.

He wants others to remember, as Dwight L. Moody, once said, "Some day you will read the papers that (I am) dead. Don't you believe a word of it. At that moment I shall be more alive than (ever). I shall have gone up higher, that is all – out of this old clay tenement into a house that is immortal; a body that death cannot touch, that sin cannot taint, a body fashioned like unto His glorious body. That which is born of the spirit will live forever." (quoted in PULPIT HELPS, March 1989, p. 15)

*Part Five:  Youth Reflection by Sara Gallegos*


*She shared the following message
at Keith's funeral on July 17, 2008.*


### *"Youth Reflection"*


I have the privilege of sharing a few of the fond memories our youth have of our Pastor Keith. I, personally, have known Pastor Keith for almost seven years; and like all who first met our individual pastor, my eyebrows raised and I was skeptical, but more than that I was curious. Over these years I have grown to love and respect the character of Rev. Keith A. McDonald.

His character was something else; we remember him for being enthusiastic about all projects, from painting windows to singing at fifth week Youth Sundays; for being crazy and totally random; for being a bit obnoxious, but making us shake with laughter; but mostly we remember him for being absolutely non-self-conscious, he did not care what people thought, he was going to be himself and have fun doing it.

Pastor Keith was forever pulling our legs. Two examples are his name and age. For the longest time we truly believed our energetic pastor was 58 years old instead of 48 years old; only after asking Yong Hui did we find out the truth. Then, during krautburger-making two years ago, Keith told us that his middle initial stood for Alfonzo. And that funny white lie, he took to the grave with him; this morning I read Pastor Keith's history; you guys have already heard… his middle name is Alan. I was shocked, but got a pretty big chuckle out of it. Speaking of laughing, one thing that all our youth will forever remember is his laugh. He got a kick out of life and shared his joy with all around him.

One time for an entire year, he wore a brown shoe and a black shoe, just to see if anyone would notice, while saying he was testing to see if the old or new was more comfortable.

We had the pleasure of being involved in many different activities with Pastor. He always participated in every church activity, a feat very difficult to be accomplished by ministers, but he always was willing to help and give everything his all. He was a very important part of our Vacation Bible School; an incredible impersonator, teacher, and always engaging the children.

This year he organized a well received "Dance Off" for our final day. He was also the founder of numerous Bible studies, open to the young and older alike. To many he will be remembered as the Bible Question Man because he once said, "Ask me any question you have about anything in the Bible, and I will be able to answer it; if you ever stump me, I will buy you lunch." Well, no one ever got a free lunch from that.

His presence at Relay for Life will be greatly missed, as he served for our all-night entertainment, from shaving his head bald, to telling ridiculous jokes (that we often fell asleep during). Oh, and his help with the Soup Supper, his wonderful oyster stews and infamous Menudo, complete with the Menudo song. Pastor Keith gave free Tae Kwon Do lessons, in which some youth had the excitement of smashing melons as he held them up, ending in a very sticky instructor. And who can forget the many sporting events that he attended and fair shows he came to, supporting and encouraging the young with all his heart and voice. Sometimes at games he would loosen up the crowd by yelling "Swing Frank, Swing" to every player during a softball game.

One of Pastor's favorite things were his dogs. Who can ever forget Bradley pulling the racing cart holding a grinning guy? Our youth group was so thrilled to join in on the adventure, and Pastor Keith even made special visits to members' houses to give rides. Of course, the dog pulling the cart wasn't shocking enough transportation, so when the cart broke down, our Pastor upgraded to the recumbent bike. Hello to a one-of-a-kind pastor as he goes pedaling down main street, Highway 52, I-76, and countless other roads.

When Keith first arrived in Keenesburg, he disliked country music; which all of us kids listen to, so in order to connect with the young people, he promptly went out and bought a Toby Keith CD, including the song, "I Wanna Talk About Me." (A song that was there after often found in his sermons on self-centeredness and selfishness.) Needless to say, he was yet to be impressed, so he bought more CDs and listened to more radio stations; while never becoming a country-western fanatic, he could carry on a conversation of any country star and quote many songs. While playing volleyball with the Hikers to Heaven, Pastor always quoted Star Trek and Star Gate before he served, giving him the power to ace us all. "Jaffa Cree" was the most famous, and Jaffa became the name of his second dog.

To do even more for the youth of the community, every Monday at noon, you would find our Pastor at the school, entertaining and talking to all who stopped by his lunch table. His noon lunches will always be remembered. During the summer we would meet with Pastor at the Rebel Express and Carl's Jr. for a youth lunch. Our final lunch date with Pastor was also the first official Chrysalis Reunion Group meeting, with five of us there we had a brief service and then started talking.

The subject of dating came up, and Amber Gustafson and I tried to explain what the terms dating, going out, being together, boyfriend, and girlfriend meant. It thoroughly confused Pastor, as we told him that dating and going out were two different things. So he asked us to define these terms and then he would use them in his devotional, so he could get the word out to all older generations.

This lasting memory makes us laugh, but also symbolizes his willingness to connect and determination to understand the youth, so he could better serve them. Being a youth leader was not something that Pastor had in his blood, but acquired through intense observation and practice; his efforts forevermore will be seen walking down the streets of our town and hallways of our school.

I would like to end with a bit of Scripture: *"There is a time for everything, and a season for every activity under heaven: a time to be born and a time to die, a time to plant and a time to uproot, a time to kill and a time to heal, a time to tear down and a time to build, a time to weep and a time to laugh, a time to mourn and a time to dance, a time to scatter stones and a time to gather them, a time to embrace and a time to refrain, a time to search and a time to give up, a time to keep and a time to throw away, a time to tear and a time to mend, a time to be silent and a time to speak, a time to love and a time to hate, a time for war and a time for peace."* *(Ecclesiastes 3:1-8)*

Now is the time for all of us to step up to fill those mismatched shoes of our dearly beloved Pastor Keith, because though they were small feet, it will take all of us to fill his shoes. From all the youth that our wild, unique pastor has impressed, we say thank you God for the blessing of your servant, Reverend Keith Alfonzo (Alan) McDonald; he will never be forgotten.

*Part Six: A 30-Day Prayer Project:*
*How to Grieve & Experience Healing from*
*the Death and Loss of Your Loved One*

By Yong Hui V. McDonald

## 1. Who needs this prayer?

If you have lost a loved one, are grieving, and want to experience healing, this project is for you. When you lose a person you love, it's like you are a leaf being blown away by a strong wind. In order to land safely from this disaster, you need healing from grief and pain. Healing is a process that involves many areas. You will be dealing with different emotions such as shock, denial, fear, frustration, anger, forgiveness, attachments, trust, faith, regrets, triggers, acceptance, idolizing the person, letting go of the person, and more. Your healing depends on how you process these areas.

The time of grieving is the time to trust God more than ever. He has the power to heal your broken heart. The Scripture tells us to *"Trust in the Lord with all your heart and lean not on your own understanding; in all your ways acknowledge him, and he will make your paths straight. Do not be wise in your own eyes; fear the Lord and shun evil. This will bring health to your body and nourishment to your bones." (Proverb 3:5-8)*

## 2. Understand the area you need healing.

Reflect on four different areas, so you will know where you need to focus. Healing is experienced with God, yourself, the deceased, and others who are involved with the death of your loved one.

(1) <u>Do you have peace with God?</u> You need to know and believe that God is good, even during the loss of your loved one. Death

and loss is a result of living in a fallen, imperfect world with frail bodies. Sometimes our loved one's tragic, sudden death may be caused by people's weaknesses and bad decisions. It's not God's doing. If you are angry with God, because you think that He caused you pain by taking your loved one, you need to work on understanding God's love. When you can accept His love and healing power, you are beginning down the path to restoration. God is for you and not against you. Jesus said, *"I have come that they may have life, and have it to the full." (John 10:10)*

(2) Do you have peace with yourself? If you had hurt the person in any way while they were alive, you need to forgive yourself. Also, you need to ask God to forgive you and accept that He does.

(3) Do you have peace with the person you have lost? You may need to take care of the issues surrounding the death of the person. You need to forgive the person that you lost, in order to find peace.

(4) Do you have peace with everyone who has anything to do with the death of your loved one? *"If it is possible, as far as it depends on you, live at peace with everyone. Do not take revenge, my friends, but leave room for God's wrath, for it is written: 'It is mine to avenge; I will repay,' says the Lord." (Romans 12:18-19)* Having peace does not mean that you have to reconcile with everyone face to face. It means you have accepted the reality of the loss, but you do not hold any resentment or anger toward anyone. **Prayer:** "Holy Spirit, guide and direct me with your wisdom and strength. Help me to do what I need to do to find peace and healing, so I can come out of this fire with strength and courage."


3. How to participate in this prayer project?

The following exercises will help you find peace as you work on different areas.

(1) Read the Bible 30 minutes every day for the next 30 days. Scripture reading and meditation bring encouragement and healing. Read Job, Psalms, Proverbs, John, and other Scripture,

to understand God's love and His healing power. You can learn from Job when you are grieving. He lost all of his seven sons, three daughters, and wealth at once. *"At this, Job got up and tore his robe and shaved his head. Then he fell to the ground in worship and said: 'Naked I came from my mother's womb, and naked I will depart. The Lord gave and the Lord has taken away; may the name of the Lord be praised.' In all this, Job did not sin by charging God with wrongdoing." (Job 1:20-22)* Job praised the Lord in his loss. He didn't blame God for his losses. All our family, friends, material things, and our lives are temporary gifts from God. Job understood that and acted on it. Read John 14:1-6, Psalm 23, Psalm 103, and Revelation 21 to understand God's plans for a better future for those who believe in Jesus. *"He will wipe every tear from their eyes. There will be no more death or mourning or crying or pain, for the old order of things has passed away." (Revelation 21:4) "Come to me, all you who are weary and burdened, and I will give you rest." (Matthew 11:28)*

(2) Pray for 30 minutes everyday for the next 30 days. Speak to God for 15 minutes and listen to God in silence for 15 minutes. It is important to express your feelings and needs to God and ask Him to help you experience healing. Also, it is important to practice listening to God in silence. When you are grieving, there are many thoughts and attitudes that need to be adjusted and cleansed. Resist any disturbing thoughts so you can listen to God's voice without distraction. **Prayer:** "I am listening to you. If there is any sin in my life for which I need to repent, please reveal it to me so I can experience healing." (2 Chronicles 7:14-15, 1 John 1:9)

(3) Resist the devil's temptation to blame God. Our mind is a spiritual battlefield. The devil can speak to our minds and plant seeds of wrong attitudes, resentment, anger, and bitterness. When we face difficult times through grief and loss, the devil will try to convince us that God doesn't care about us. When people blame God for their losses, they want to turn away. (1 Peter 5:6-9) God cared enough to give His only Son, Jesus, to die for our sins. (John 3:16-17)

(4) <u>Write a prayer or letter to God</u>. Write a letter of questions, wishes, pain, acceptance, releasing, and letting go of your loved one. **Prayer**: "Lord Jesus, I give my fears, desires, plans, and unforgiving spirit to you. Take away the desire to hold on to my loved one. Please heal my heart in Jesus' name. Amen."

(5) <u>Focus on God's blessings and grace instead of your loss</u>. Read, meditate, and memorize Psalm 23:5-6 and make it your prayer whenever you are hurting: *"You prepare a table before me in the presence of my enemies. You anoint my head with oil; my cup overflows. Surely goodness and love will follow me all the days of my life, and I will dwell in the house of the Lord forever."*

(6) <u>Develop an attitude of gratefulness; praise God for what He has given you</u>. Paul wrote, *"We also rejoice in our sufferings, because we know that suffering produces perseverance; perseverance, character; and character, hope. And hope does not disappoint us, because God has poured out his love into our hearts by the Holy Spirit, whom he has given us. You see, at just the right time, when we were still powerless, Christ died for the ungodly." (Romans 5:3-6)* We can praise God in any circumstances by focusing on God's grace.

(7) <u>Forgive everyone including yourself</u>. You need to let go of all resentment, anger, and bitterness toward anyone (including yourself) associated with your loved one's death. One by one, tell God that you forgive your loved one or others who are involved. **Prayer**: "God, I release all my anger, resentment, bitterness, and my unforgiving spirit. Take away all of my thoughts that are hindering the healing process of my soul and spirit. Please forgive me, if I have sinned against you and others. I forgive everyone who is responsible for my loved one's death. Bless them and forgive them, as you have blessed me and forgiven me." (1 Matthew 5:44, John 4:20)

(8) <u>Have compassion for yourself and others who may be related to the death of your loved one</u>.

(9) <u>Start a journal to express your pain, feelings of hurt, restoration and how God is helping you</u>.

(10) <u>Write a letter to your loved one</u>. Write a love letter, forgiveness letter, releasing letter, or good-bye letter to your loved one. (Philippians 4:4-8)

(11) <u>To help others, write a testimony or book about how God is helping you in your grieving process</u>. (Revelation 12:11) *"Those who sow in tears will reap with songs of joy. He who goes out weeping, carrying seed to sow, will return with songs of joy, carrying sheaves with him." (Psalm 126:5)*

(12) <u>Let go of self-pity</u>. Don't expect others to understand your pain and meet your needs. Many people do not know how to help those who are grieving. By letting go of your expectations of how others should help you, you will be freed from a critical and judgmental spirit. (Matthew 7:1-5)

(13) <u>Let go of your loved one</u>. You have to grieve. It is necessary so that you can experience healing in different areas. But, if you decide to grieve for the rest of your life, you will be immobilized by the pain. Your relationship with God will also suffer, because your grieving will become a distraction. You have to let your loved one go, in order to experience healing. **Prayer:** "God, I am giving you all of my desires, wishes, dreams, regrets, and unforgiving spirit associated with my loved one. Please take away any painful memories as well as my desire to be with my loved one. In Jesus' name I pray. Amen."

(14) <u>Ask God to heal you from triggers of grief and pain</u>. You will learn what makes you break down in pain when you lose someone. You may need to put away the items that trigger your grief and pain. However, you cannot put away everything since anything can be a trigger. The ultimate healing will come from the Lord when you put God first and not the person you have lost. **Prayer:** "Lord Jesus, you are my joy and my love. I ask you to heal me so that I don't suffer from any triggers. I love you more than anyone and anything. Please help me focus my heart on you so grieving does not become a distraction between you and me. Amen." (Matthew 7:7, Colossians 3:1-4)

(15) <u>Ask Jesus to anoint you for healing</u>. Put your hand on your head and ask, "Lord Jesus, I am hurting. Please touch me and

heal my troubled mind, heart, soul, and spirit. Holy Spirit, fill my heart with your peace and joy, and bring healing. Heavenly Father, I praise you for helping me in my troubled times."

(16) <u>Pray for healing of painful memories</u>. Here is a prayer for those who experienced a tragic death of a loved one. **Prayer:** "Lord Jesus, please heal my memories of the painful death of my loved one. I can let go of my resentment, bitterness, and anger, so I can forgive and have peace of mind."

(17) <u>When you can, do something to forget about your loss</u>. Take a break to enjoy small things in life – nature, drawing, exercise, dancing, or even humor. Don't turn to alcohol, drugs, violence, or follow destructive sinful paths to avoid the pain. When you do that, it will delay healing and the end result can be devastating.

(18) <u>Find supportive friends who will listen and understand your situation, struggles, and feelings</u>.

(19) <u>Join a grief support group or start one if you can't find one</u>. Find people who will join this prayer project for 30 days. Discuss your loss, what you need to do to experience healing, how you are making progress, and how God is helping you. Pray for each other's healing. *"Is any one of you in trouble? He should pray. Is anyone happy? Let him sing songs of praise. Is any one of you sick? He should call the elders of the church to pray over him and anoint him with oil in the name of the Lord. And the prayer offered in faith will make the sick person well; the Lord will raise him up. If he has sinned, he will be forgiven. Therefore confess your sins to each other and pray for each other so that you may be healed. The prayer of a righteous man is powerful and effective." (James 5:13-16)*

(20) <u>Help others who are hurting</u>. As you help others, your pain will start to look small. You will see that you are not alone. There are many who carry more pain than you do. (Galatians 6:2)

(21) <u>If you do not have a relationship with Jesus, this is an opportunity to invite Him into your heart</u>. **Prayer:** "Lord Jesus, I invite you into my heart and my life. I give my heart to you. Forgive all my sins and wash me. Lord, I am hurting, but I believe that you can heal my broken heart. Fill my heart with

your joy and peace. If there is any area that I need to work on, please teach me what I need to do." (Romans 10:10-11)

(22)Attend church to get to know God and to experience love, support, and healing. (Hebrews 10:25)


## 4. What happens as you experience healing from grief caused by loss?

When you are healed, you are not immersed in grief and pain from your loss. Your heart is filled with gratitude, thankfulness, and compassion toward others who are hurting. Also, you will be free from triggers of grief and pain, and be able to function normally. You will be amazed at how much God can bring healing to your broken heart.

You will learn to be content with what you have. *"I can do everything through him who gives me strength." (Philippians 4:13)* Your heart will be filled with the hope God has for you. *"But now, Lord, what do I look for? My hope is in you." (Psalm 39:7)* You will know that God comforts those who are hurting. *"Praise be to the God and Father of our Lord Jesus Christ, the Father of compassion and the God of all comfort, who comforts us in all our troubles, so that we can comfort those in any trouble with the comfort we ourselves have received from God." (2 Corinthians 1:3-4)*

*"The Lord will surely comfort Zion and will look with compassion on all her ruins; he will make her deserts like Eden, her wastelands like the garden of the Lord. Joy and gladness will be found in her, thanksgiving and the sound of singing." (Isaiah 51:3)*

*"But he was pierced for our transgressions, he was crushed for our iniquities; the punishment that brought us peace was upon him, and by his wounds we are healed." (Isaiah 53:5)*

*"When you pass through the water, I will be with you; and when you pass through the rivers, they will not sweep over you. When you walk through the fire, you will not be burned; the flames will not set you ablaze." (Isaiah 43:2)*

## Part Seven: Invitations

### 1. An Invitation to accept Christ

Do you have an empty heart that cannot be filled with anyone or anything? God can fill your empty heart with His love and forgiveness. Do you feel your life has no meaning, no direction, no purpose, and you don't know where to turn to find the answers? It's time to turn to God because that's the only way you can understand the meaning and purpose of your life. You will find a direction that will lead you to fulfillment and joy. Is your heart broken and hurting, and you don't know how to experience healing? Until we meet Christ in our hearts, we cannot find the peace and healing that God can provide. Jesus can help heal your broken heart. If you don't have a relationship with Christ, this is an opportunity for you to accept Jesus into your heart so you can be saved, find peace and healing from God. Here is a prayer if you are ready to accept Jesus.

"Dear Jesus, I surrender my life and everything to you. I give you all my pain, fear, regret, resentment, anger, worry, and concerns that overwhelm me. I am a sinner. I need your forgiveness. Please come into my heart and my life and forgive all my sins. I believe that you died for my sins and that you have plans for my life. Please heal my broken heart and bless me with your peace and joy. Help me to cleanse my life so I can live a godly life. Help me to understand your plans for my life and help me to obey you. Fill me with the Holy Spirit, and guide me so I can follow your way. I pray this in Jesus' name. Amen."

*Dancing in the Sky*

## 2. An Invitation for The Transformation Project Prison Ministry (TPPM).

Chaplain Yong Hui V. McDonald has been in prison ministry since 1999. She started working as a chaplain at Adams County Detention Facility (ACDF) in Brighton, Colorado, in 2003. She started the Transformation Project Prison Ministry (TPPM) in 2005 in an effort to bring spiritually nurturing books to the inmates at the facility because the chaplains' office had a shortage of inspirational books. In the process, Maximum Saints books and DVDs were produced by ACDF inmates for the other inmates.

Maximum Saints are not necessary classified as maximum security inmates; they are called Maximum Saints because they are using their gifts to the maximum to help others.

The Maximum Saints books and DVDs project provides the ACDF incarcerated saints an opportunity and offers encouragement to put their writing and artistic skills to use to provide hope, peace, restoration, and healing. It also gives spiritual support to incarcerated people, the homeless, as well as to interested persons outside the prisons.

TPPM is committed to help those who are spiritually hungry and need Christ's message. Within five years, TPPM produced seven English books, two Spanish books and four DVDs. This year, *Maximum Saints Dream* book was published and currently TPPM is working on a book and DVD on forgiveness.

Books and DVDs produced by TPPM are distributed in many jails, prisons, and homeless shelters nationwide free of charge made possible by grants and donations. America has 2.3 million people incarcerated, the largest prison population in the world, and there is a great shortage of inspirational books in many jails and prisons.

## "One Million Dream Project"

In 2010, TPPM board decided to expand the ministry goal and started, "One Million Dream Project." TPPM decided to raise enough funds to distribute one million copies of each book TPPM produced for prisoners and homeless people. I ask you to pray for this project so God can help TPPM to reach out to those who cannot speak for themselves but are in need of spiritual guidance from the Lord.

TPPM is a 501 (c) (3) non-profit organization so your donation is 100% tax deductible. TPPM is an Advance of the United Methodist Church with Advance #3020547. If you would like to be a partner in this very important mission of bringing transformation through the message of Christ in prisons and homeless shelters or want to know more about this project, go to the website: www.transformprisons.org. You can donate on line or you can write a check addressed to: Transformation Project Prison Ministry and send it to the following address: Transformation Project Prison Ministry

5209 Montview Boulevard
Denver, CO 80207
303-655-3311 or 720-951-2629

Website: www.transformprisons.org
You can find Transformation Project Prison Ministry on facebook.

The book, *Dancing in the Sky, A Story of Hope for Grieving Hearts* is distributed in jails, prisons and homeless shelters nationwide free of charge made possible by grants and donations.